Cambridge English
First
Result

Student's Book

Paul A Davies & Tim Falla

OXFORD
UNIVERSITY PRESS

Contents

Introduction

About this course

This fully updated and revised edition provides preparation and practice for candidates who are preparing for the 2015 *Cambridge English: First (FCE)* exam. The material also provides opportunities for learners to develop their English on a broader level for success in the real world beyond the exam.

The units in this **Student's Book** contain practice of exam-type tasks for each part of the exam. Vocabulary and grammar practice are also an integral part of the course. The *Writing Guide* and *Grammar Reference* at the back of the book provide additional support to consolidate the language and skills covered in the main units.

Interactive online materials help to build on and extend the language and skills covered in the Student's Book and Workbook. The **Online Practice** (your unique access code is on the card at the back of this book) contains additional material which includes:

- exam practice tasks for each part of the exam, including speak-and-record tasks
- skills training exercises
- access to the *Oxford Advanced Learner's Dictionary 8th Edition**
- feedback on your answers*

(*available for self-study use or if your teacher sets assignments from the Online Practice 'with help')

The access code for your Online Practice also gives you access to a **complete online practice test** with feedback on your answers.

A **Workbook** with audio CD provides further exam, language, and skills practice and access to **another complete online practice test**.

We hope that you enjoy using this book to help you prepare for the *Cambridge English: First (FCE)* exam.

About the exam

Cambridge English: First (FCE) is an upper-intermediate level qualification targeted at level B2 on the CEFR scale. It is proof that a candidate is becoming skilled in English, and it is widely used by learners who want to study, live, or work in an English-speaking environment. It is officially recognized by a number of organizations around the world, including universities, employers, and governments. For more information on recognition, go to www.cambridgeenglish.org/recognition.

Revisions to the *Cambridge English: First (FCE)* exam for 2015 have been made to ensure that it continues to meet the needs and expectations of candidates, teachers, and other users. The revisions also reflect the latest methodological approaches to communicative language testing.

The revised *Cambridge English: First (FCE)* exam for 2015 consists of four papers:
- **Reading and Use of English** (1 hour and 15 minutes)
- **Writing** (1 hour and 20 minutes)
- **Listening** (approx. 40 minutes)
- **Speaking** (approx. 14 minutes)

The exam takes approximately 3 hours and 30 minutes.

For more details and the most up-to-date information about the 2015 *Cambridge English: First (FCE)* exam, go to www.cambridgeenglish.org.

Exam overview

Paper 1 Reading and Use of English (1 hour 15 minutes)

This paper has seven parts. Parts 1 to 4 have texts with accompanying grammar and vocabulary tasks, and discrete items with a grammar and vocabulary focus. Parts 5 to 7 have texts and accompanying reading comprehension tasks.

Part	Task type	Number of items	What you do	What it tests	How to do it
1	Multiple-choice cloze	8	Fill 8 gaps in a text, choosing from four-option multiple-choice items.	Phrases, collocations, linkers, used to complete a text with the correct meaning and grammatical context.	page 89
2	Open cloze	8	Fill 8 gaps in a text with one word per gap.	Your awareness and control of structural items.	page 28
3	Word formation	8	Form appropriate words from prompts to complete 8 gaps in a text.	Word formation	page 64
4	Key word transformations	6	Complete a gapped sentence with two to five words, including a key word, so that it has the same meaning as the lead-in sentence.	Your awareness and control of grammatical and lexical items.	page 112
5	Multiple choice	6	Choose the best answer from four-option multiple-choice questions	Your understanding of a text and opinions expressed in it.	page 10
6	Gapped text	6	Decide where sentences belong in a text.	Your understanding of text structure and development	page 94
7	Multiple matching	10	Match prompts from a list to elements in a text.	Your ability to find specific information.	page 22

Marks

Parts 1 to 3: one mark for each correct answer

Part 4: up to two marks for each correct answer

Parts 5 and 6: two marks for each correct answer

Part 7: one mark for each correct answer

Paper 2 Writing (1 hour 20 minutes)

This paper has two parts. The Part 1 question is a compulsory essay, and is based on input information. In Part 2 you choose one question from three.

Answers for Part 1 and Part 2 should be 140–190 words in length.

The task types for Part 2 will be from the following: article, email/letter, report, review.

Examples of question types can be found in the Writing Guide on pages 155–161.

Part	Task type	Number of items	What you do	What it tests	How to do it
1	Compulsory contextualized task based on input material of up to 120 words, in the form of an essay title to respond to, with accompanying notes to guide your writing.	One compulsory task.	Write an essay, according to the task instructions.	Your ability to outline and discuss issues on a particular topic.	page 31
2	Contextualized task in no more than 70 words.	One from a choice of three questions.	Write, according to the task instructions.	Your ability to write according to the instructions, in the correct style, layout and register in order to have a positive effect on the reader.	page 19 page 43 page 55 page 67 page 91 page 127

Marks

Parts 1 and 2 have equal marks.

Paper 3 Listening (approx. 40 minutes)

This paper has four parts, and 30 questions.

The recorded texts may include the following:

Monologues: lectures, talks, presentations, anecdotes, radio broadcasts, etc.

Conversations between two or three speakers: conversations, interviews, discussions, etc.

The testing focus is on understanding specific information, gist, attitude, opinion, main points and detail.

All parts are heard twice. The instructions are given on the question paper. The recordings include a variety of voices, styles of delivery and accents.

Part	Task type	Number of items	What you do	What it tests	How to do it
1	Multiple choice	8	Listen to eight unrelated extracts and choose the best answer from three-option multiple-choice items.	Your understanding of gist, detail, function, purpose, attitude, situation, genre, etc.	page 50
2	Sentence completion	10	Listen to a monologue and complete gaps in sentences with information from the text.	Your understanding of detail, specific information, stated opinion.	page 110
3	Multiple matching	5	Listen to five short related monologues and select the correct option from a list of eight.	As Part 1.	page 98
4	Multiple choice	7	Listen to a text involving two interacting speakers and choose the best answer from three-option multiple-choice items.	Your understanding of opinion, attitude, gist, main idea, specific information.	page 14

Marks

One mark for each correct answer.

Spelling must be correct for common words and those considered easy to spell.

Paper 4 Speaking (approx. 14 minutes)

This paper has four parts.

The standard format is two candidates and two examiners, one acting as interlocutor and assessor, the other acting as assessor only. In certain circumstances, three candidates may sit the test together.

Part	Task type	Length	What you do	What it tests	How to do it
1	A short conversation between the interlocutor and each candidate.	3 minutes	Ask and answer 'personal' questions,	Your ability to use general interactional and social language.	page 15
2	Individual long turns and brief responses.	1 minute long turn for each candidate and 20-second response from the second candidate.	Talk about visual prompts	Your ability to describe, compare, express opinions.	page 123
3	Two-way interaction between candidates.	3 minutes	Discuss and do a decision-making task based on written prompts.	Your ability to exchange ideas, express and justify opinions, agree and disagree, speculate, evaluate and reach a decision through negotiation, etc.	page 39
4	A discussion between candidates and the interlocutor.	4 minutes	Discuss issues related to the Part 3 topic.	Your ability to express and justify opinions, agree and/or disagree.	page 87

Marks

Candidates are assessed on their performance throughout the test in the following areas:

- Grammar and vocabulary (accuracy and appropriacy)
- Discourse management (ability to express ideas in coherent, connected speech)
- Pronunciation (individual sounds, linking of words, stress and intonation)
- Interactive communication (turn-taking, initiating and responding)
- Global achievement (overall effectiveness in the tasks)

The assessor marks according to detailed Analytical Scales, the interlocutor gives a mark on a Global Scale, which is less detailed.

The circle of life

Lead in

1 Name any of the people you recognize in the photos. Guess who is related and what the relationships are.

2 Compare your answers to 1 in pairs. Say which physical features a–g helped you to guess.

   a skin tone (fair/dark/tanned)
   b hair colour (black/fair/blond/red)
   c hairstyle (curly/straight)
   d eye colour (blue/green/hazel/brown)
   e eyebrows (bushy/thin)
   f nose (large/small/hooked/turned up)
   g mouth (full/thin lips)

3 Turn to page 153 to find out the answers to 1.

4 Work in pairs. Find out from your partner whether

   • they look like one or both parents.
   • they look like another relative in some way.
   • they have a similar personality to a parent or sibling (brother or sister).

Reading

Part 5 Multiple choice

1 Would you like to have an identical twin? What advantages and disadvantages might there be?

2 Read the text opposite quickly. What do cases like the 'Jim twins' tell scientists: a, b or c?

   a why some women give birth to identical twins

   b which physical features we inherit from which parent

   c how much of our personality we inherit from our parents

how to do it

Read the text quickly for general meaning.

Read the questions first. Don't read the options (A–D) yet.

Underline the parts of the text that contain the information you need.

Read the options and look again at the relevant part of the text. Cross out any options that are clearly wrong.

If you can't decide between two options, make an intelligent guess.

3 Read the **how to do it** box. Then read the text again carefully, and for questions 1–6, choose the answer (A, B, C or D) which you think fits best, according to the text.

1 Unlike non-identical twins, identical twins
  A are more common among Asians than Africans.
  B are becoming more and more common.
  C are more common among older mothers.
  D are no more frequent in one geographical area than another.

2 Scientists are particularly interested in identical twins who
  A have been raised by different families.
  B haven't been studied before.
  C look and behave in very similar ways.
  D are not alike in terms of personality.

3 While they were growing up, twins Jim Lewis and Jim Springer
  A were in regular contact.
  B knew about their twin, but had no contact.
  C did not know they had ever had a twin.
  D were prevented from seeing each other by their adoptive families.

4 When the two Jims met as adults, how did they react to the similarities between them?
  A They had always expected them.
  B They found them very amusing.
  C They did not realize how similar they were until the researchers told them.
  D They were very surprised.

5 As adults, the twins
  A both had only one child.
  B each had two wives.
  C had pets with the same name.
  D married women who were identical twins.

6 How do other cases of twins raised apart compare with the 'Jim twins'?
  A They are all just as surprising.
  B They are less surprising, but often show interesting coincidences.
  C Many of them are even more surprising.
  D Most of them show that other pairs of identical twins are not very similar.

THE JIM TWINS

You take it for granted that you are a unique person, different from everybody else on Earth, and you understand that everybody else is also unique. Identical twins are fascinating because they
5 challenge this notion: they are unique people, of course, but they're also unnervingly similar to each other – and not only in terms of appearance. They often share opinions, mannerisms and personality traits.

Identical twins are rare, occurring
10 in about three out of every 1,000 births. They seem to occur at random, regardless of the age or ethnic background of the mother (unlike non-identical twins which are, for
15 example, far more common among Africans than Asians). Although there may be tiny differences in physical appearances between two identical twins, which allow family and close
20 friends to tell them apart, they do have exactly the same DNA. This is because they develop from a single egg, which divides in two during the very early stages of pregnancy.

25 For most scientists, it's the non-physical similarities between identical twins that are the most interesting: are they the result of growing up together in the same home, or are they the result of their identical
30 DNA? By studying identical twins who have not grown up together, researchers can see which similarities remain and which disappear. In other words, they can learn which aspects of a person's identity are determined by genes and which are influenced by the environment. The
35 Minnesota Twin Study is probably the best-known twin study to date. The study provides information about how our environment and genes work together to influence everything from attitudes, talents and abilities, to job selection, falling in love, aging and health.

40 Identical twins Jim Lewis and Jim Springer were only four weeks old when they were separated; each infant was taken in by a different adoptive family. At age five, Lewis learned that he had a twin, but he said that the idea never truly 'soaked in' until he was 38 years old.
45 Springer learned of his twin at age eight, but both he and his adoptive parents believed the brother had died. The two Jims were finally reunited at age 39.

The similarities the twins shared not only amazed each other, but also amazed researchers at the University of
50 Minnesota. The very fact that both twins were given the same name was a big coincidence. But there's more:

- As youngsters, each Jim had a dog named 'Toy'.
- Each Jim had been married twice – the first wives were both called Linda and the second wives were
55 both called Betty.
- One Jim had named his son James Allan and the other Jim had named his son James Alan.
- Each twin had driven his light-blue Chevrolet to the same beach in Florida for family vacations.
60 • Both Jims had at one time held part-time posts as sheriffs.
- Both were fingernail biters and suffered from migraine headaches.

While not as eerily similar as the Jim twins, many more
65 instances of strange likenesses can be found among twins who were raised apart. For example, identical twins Tom Patterson and Steve Tazumi had very different upbringings. Raised in a Christian family by two janitors in rural Kansas, Tom still managed to choose the same
70 career as his brother, Steve, who lives in Philadelphia and was raised in a Buddhist household. Both men own body-building gyms.

It's obvious from these twins' stories that genetics are a major factor in shaping who we are. In fact, research so
75 far indicates that characteristics such as personality are mainly related to genes. This means that our character traits as adults are largely determined before we are born – and there is very little that we, or anybody else, can do to change them.

4 Discuss your reaction to the final sentence in the text, giving reasons. Do you believe it, and if so, do you think it is a good or bad thing?

tip In the Reading and Use of English Paper you have 1 hour 15 minutes to complete 7 sections. Make sure you don't spend too much time on each section. If you don't know or can't guess an answer, move on and come back to it if you have time at the end.

Vocabulary

Describing personality

1 In pairs, discuss whether the personality adjectives in the box below are

a   good
b   bad
c   either good or bad

argumentative [b]   arrogant [b]   bossy [c]   easy-going [c]
eccentric [a]   honest [a]   loyal [a]   narrow-minded [b]
open-minded [a]   sensible [a]   sensitive [a]

2 ▶1 Listen to five people describing a friend or relative. Choose the best adjective from 1 to sum up their description.

Speaker 1 thinks that her uncle is _narrow-minded_

Speaker 2 thinks that his brother is _arrogant_ .

Speaker 3 thinks that her friend is _eccentric_ .

Speaker 4 thinks that her cousin is _bossy_ .

Speaker 5 thinks that his father is _honest_ .

3 Read the **tip** box then think of three people you know well and describe them to a partner. Use adjectives from 1 and give examples of their behaviour.

Example   My sister, Belinda, is very sensible. For example, she always goes to bed early if she has a busy day the next day.

> **tip**   You may be asked to describe somebody's character in Writing Part 2 or Speaking Part 1. When we use personality adjectives to describe somebody, we often use them with modifying adverbs like *very, a bit, rather, quite*, etc.

Grammar

Talking about the future GR p165

1 Choose the best verb form (a–c) to complete sentences 1–7.

1   By the time we get to the nightclub, most people __C__ home.
    a   will go
    b   are going
    c   will have gone

2   The train to London __b__ at 6.13, so let's meet at the station at 6 o'clock.
    a   is going to leave
    b   leaves
    c   is leaving

3   As soon as I save enough money, __b__ you a laptop.
    a   I buy
    b   I'll buy
    c   I'll have bought

4   By the time she leaves music school, she __C__ the piano for 12 years.
    a   will study
    b   will be studying
    c   will have been studying

5   Louis won't be at school tomorrow because __a__ in a swimming tournament.
    a   he's taking part
    b   he'll take part
    c   he takes part

6   This time next month, we __C__ around Thailand.
    a   will travel
    b   are travelling
    c   will be travelling

7   My sister doesn't feel well, so __C__ at home this afternoon.
    a   she'll have stayed
    b   she stays
    c   she's going to stay

2015
2020
2025

2 Complete sentences a–g with the tenses below, and match them with the sentences in 1. Check your answers in the Grammar Reference.

future continuous ✓ future perfect simple ✓
future perfect continuous ✓ *going to* future ✓
present continuous ✓ present simple ✓ *will* future ✓

a We use the _present continuous_ to talk about things that we've arranged to do in the future.

b We use the _going to_ to talk about things that we've personally decided to do in the future.

c We use the _will_ to make offers and promises and predictions.

d We use the _future continuous_ to talk about actions in progress in the future.

e We use the _future perfect simple_ to talk about completed actions in the future.

f We use the _present simple_ to talk about future events that are part of a schedule or timetable.

g We use the _future perfect continuous_ to say how long future actions will have been in progress.

3 Work in pairs. Tell your partner about something that

a humans can't do now but you think they'll be able to do by 2050.

b takes place next summer.

c exists today but will have disappeared by the year 2050, in your opinion.

d you're going to do as soon as you can afford it.

e you're doing next week.

4 Read the dialogue below. Underline any verb forms that you think are unnatural and replace them with better alternatives.

Martin Hi, is Jacqui there?

Lucy Yes, she is. Wait a moment, I'm just getting her.

Martin Thanks!

Jacqui Hi, it's Jacqui here.

Martin This is Martin. Listen carefully, I haven't got much time. Can you meet me at the port in one hour? The next boat to Tripoli will leave at 7.35.

Jacqui I can't! I'll have dinner with some people from work this evening. I've just arranged it.

Martin But we must leave tonight! By tomorrow, the newspapers are going to get hold of the story. We won't have been able to move without attracting attention.

Jacqui What story? Are you telling me what's going on?

Martin I explain everything as soon as we'll get to Tripoli. Trust me.

Jacqui Can't you explain now?

Martin There's no time. But if you don't do as I say, then by this time tomorrow, every journalist in town will knock at your door.

5 Read these predictions, ignoring the underlining. Say which ones you believe are true or false for you. Give reasons.

a I don't think I'll ever appear on television.

b I reckon I'll write a novel one day.

c I don't imagine I'll be earning much money in five years' time.

d I guess I'll be living in this town in ten years' time.

6 In pairs, talk about your ideas for your future using the questions below. Try to use some of the underlined phrases from 5 in your answers.

a Do you think you'll ever
   • experience space travel?
   • work abroad?
   • have a face-lift?
   • become a politician?
   • own a Ferrari?

b In five years' and 25 years' time, what kind of
   • house will you be living in?
   • clothes will you be wearing?
   • hobbies will you be doing?
   • holiday will you be going on?
   • job will you be doing?

Listening

Part 4 Multiple choice

1 Imagine that scientists could develop an 'immortality pill' that allowed people to live for ever. Discuss these questions.

a Would you take it? Why/Why not?

b Would you want everyone to take it? Why/Why not?

how to do it

You will have one minute to look at the questions. Read as much as you can in that time.

As you listen for the first time, mark the options that you think are correct.

Use the second listening to check your answers.

2 ▶2 You will hear an excerpt from a radio programme about living for ever. Read the **how to do it** box, then listen and choose the best answer for 1–7.

1 According to some scientists, technology that allows people to live for thousands of years

A already exists.

B will exist within 30 years.

C will be causing arguments 30 years from now.

2 According to the speaker, why are scientists closer to finding this technology?

A They are beginning to understand why and how our bodies age.

B Medical technology is improving quickly.

C There are more old people in our societies.

3 Some people argue that immortality would have a negative effect on our planet because

A we would soon use up all the earth's natural resources.

B everybody would stop caring about the environment.

C the earth would become very overcrowded.

4 What might people have to agree to do, before they would be allowed to live for ever?

A suggest ways of dealing with over-population

B not have too many children

C not commit any serious crimes

5 If you were immortal, you might find it difficult to get up in the morning because

A you would be exhausted after thousands of other mornings.

B you would know there were going to be many more mornings.

C the technology that kept you alive might make you very weak.

6 Some people say that immortality would be pointless because

A only the very rich would be able to afford it.

B you wouldn't use your time carefully.

C you would only remember a part of your life.

7 You might never fall in love if you were immortal because

A the most powerful human feelings come from knowing that we will not be here for ever.

B you would get bored with everybody that you've met.

C the technology would change the way in which your brain experiences emotions.

3 Discuss what age you would choose to be if you could stay the same age for ever. Give reasons. Think about the following.

- appearance
- daily routine
- independence
- health
- wealth
- wisdom

Speaking

Part 1

1 Read questions a–f below, then match each one with a pair of words (1–6) that you might hear in the answer.

  a Do you enjoy spending time alone? (Why/Why not?)

  b What do you use the Internet for?

  c Tell me about a close friend.

  d Tell me about the most beautiful place you have ever visited.

  e Tell me about something you found difficult but managed to succeed in.

  f What's your favourite TV programme and why?

  1 research downloading
  2 scenery spectacular
  3 dramas plot
  4 share solitary
  5 easy-going loyal
  6 satisfying achievement

2 3 Listen to six different students answering the questions in 1. Put questions a–f in the order that you hear the answers, using the words you matched them with to help you.

  1 ....   4 ....
  2 ....   5 ....
  3 ....   6 ....

3 Choose the correct word to complete these phrases from the listening in 2. Then say whether each phrase shows the end of an answer or a contrast.

  a … *from/in* my view, anyway.

  b Having said *it/that*, …

  c That's my *opinion/thought*, anyway.

  d But on *another/the other* hand …

  e So, *at/in* short …

  f But at the *one/same* time, …

  g Although I must *admit/advise* that …

  h And that's about *it/that*, really.

  i So all *for/in* all …

4 Write two questions on each of these topics.

  a future plans
  b family
  c daily routine
  d where you live

5 Read the **how to do it** box, and in pairs ask and answer questions from 1 and 4.

how to do it

Listen carefully to the question and try to repeat at least one of the key words in your reply.

Speak clearly and look at the person you are talking to.

Try to include some set phrases like the ones in 3.

Use of English

Part 4 Key word transformations

1 Read the **tip** box below, then match the underlined phrases in sentences a–f with 1–6.

a More than 200 countries will <u>take part in</u> the next Olympic Games.

b When preparing for a hike, it's important to <u>take into account</u> what the weather will be like.

c At the age of one, a baby is just starting to <u>make sense of</u> the world around him.

d Marianne agreed to be home by midnight because she didn't want to <u>have a row</u> with her parents.

e It's arrogant to <u>make fun of</u> other people's achievements.

f Several factors <u>play a part in</u> the success or failure of a film.

1	argue *d*	4	laugh at *e*
2	consider *b*	5	join in *a*
3	be a cause of *f*	6	understand *c*

tip Phrases like those underlined in 1 usually appear in dictionaries under the noun rather than the verb. You may have to read the entry carefully to find them.

2 Using a dictionary, find verbs to replace 1–6 in the text below.

Last weekend, I organized an 80th birthday party for my grandfather. Two of my brothers agreed to [1]<u>lend a hand</u> with the preparations. Our sister Rachel was out of the country at the time. My grandfather has so many grandchildren now, he sometimes [2]<u>loses track of</u> their names, but Rachel has always been a favourite. I [3]<u>let her know</u> about the party, and she [4]<u>got in touch with</u> our grandfather on the day to [5]<u>say sorry</u> for not being there. She [6]<u>gave him her word</u> that she would visit him as soon as she returned home.

1. give a hand / help
2. don't remember
3. Informed
4. be in contact
5. apologise
6. promises

3 Rewrite each sentence a–f keeping the meaning the same. Use two to five words including the word given.

a Students at the summer school are expected to participate in leisure activities.
   part
   Students at the summer school are expected to _take part in_ leisure activities.

b Stubborn people often find it difficult to apologize for their mistakes.
   sorry
   Stubborn people often find it difficult _to say sorry for_ their mistakes.

c Considering that my grandmother is so old, her memory is amazing.
   account _take into_
   If you _account how_ old my grandmother is, her memory is amazing.

d Contacting a doctor on a Sunday can be difficult.
   touch
   It can be difficult to _get in touch_ with a doctor on a Sunday.

e When he first moved to London, some of the children at school used to laugh at his accent.
   make
   When he first moved to London, some of the children at school used to _make fun of_ his accent.

f When she invited us for dinner, we promised that we wouldn't be late.
   word
   When she invited us for dinner, we _gave her our word_ that we wouldn't be late.

Vocabulary

Using a dictionary

belt 0̶ /belt/ *noun, verb*
- *noun* **1** 0̶ a long narrow piece of leather, cloth, etc. that you wear around the waist: *to do up/fasten/tighten a belt* ◊ *a belt buckle* ➔ VISUAL VOCAB page V51 ➔ see also BLACK BELT, LIFEBELT, SEAT BELT, SUSPENDER BELT **2** a continuous band of material that moves round and is used to carry things along or to drive machinery ➔ see also CONVEYOR BELT, FAN BELT **3** an area with particular characteristics or where a particular group of people live: *the country's corn/industrial belt* ◊ *We live in the commuter belt.* ◊ *a belt of rain moving across the country* ➔ see also GREEN BELT **4** (*informal*) an act of hitting sth/sb hard: *She gave the ball a terrific belt.*
- **IDM** **below the 'belt** (of a remark) unfair or cruel: *That was distinctly below the belt!* ˌbelt and 'braces (*informal*) taking more actions than are really necessary to make sure that sth succeeds or works as it should: *a belt-and-braces policy* **have sth under your 'belt** (*informal*) to have already achieved or obtained sth: *She already has a couple of good wins under her belt.* ➔ more at TIGHTEN
- *verb* **1** ~ sb/sth (*informal*) to hit sb/sth hard: *He belted the ball right out of the park.* ◊ *I'll belt you if you do that again.* **2** [I] + adv./prep. (*informal, especially BrE*) to move very fast **SYN** tear: *A truck came belting up behind us.* **3** [T] ~ sth to fasten a belt around sth: *The dress was belted at the waist.*
- **PHRV** ˌbelt sth↔'out (*informal*) to sing a song or play music loudly ˌbelt 'up (*BrE*) **1** (*NAmE* ˌbuckle 'up) (*informal*) to fasten your SEAT BELT (= a belt worn by a passenger in a vehicle) **2** (*informal*) used to tell sb rudely to be quiet **SYN** shut up: *Just belt up, will you!*

pale 0̶ /peɪl/ *adj., verb, noun*
- *adj.* (**paler, pal·est**) **1** 0̶ (of a person, their face, etc.) having skin that is almost white; having skin that is whiter than usual because of illness, a strong emotion, etc: *a pale complexion* ◊ *pale with fear* ◊ *to go/turn pale* ◊ *You look pale. Are you OK?* ◊ *The ordeal left her looking pale and drawn.* **2** 0̶ light in colour; containing a lot of white: *pale blue eyes* ◊ *a paler shade of green* ◊ *a pale sky* **OPP** dark, deep **3** 0̶ (of light) not strong or bright: *the cold pale light of dawn* ➔ see also PALLID, PALLOR ▸ **pale·ly** /'peɪlli/ *adv.*: *Mark stared palely* (= with a pale face) *at his plate.* **pale·ness** *noun* [U]
- *verb* [I] ~ (at sth) to become paler than usual: *She* (= her face) *paled visibly at the sight of the police car.* ◊ *The blue of the sky paled to a light grey.*
- **IDM** 'pale beside/next to sth | 'pale in/by comparison (with/to sth) | 'pale into insignificance to seem less important when compared with sth else: *Last year's riots pale in comparison with this latest outburst of violence.*
- *noun*
- **IDM** be·ˌyond the 'pale considered by most people to be unacceptable or unreasonable: *His remarks were clearly beyond the pale.*

Oxford Advanced Learner's Dictionary, 8th edition

1 Read the two dictionary entries opposite. Find at least one example of a–h.

- a a synonym (a word with the same meaning)
- b an opposite
- c an idiom
- d a meaning which only exists in British English
- e an American English equivalent
- f an informal expression
- g a phrasal verb
- h an impolite expression

2 Match the underlined words in a–f with the relevant part of the dictionary entries. Give the part of speech and number.

- a NASA is planning to send a probe to explore the asteroid <u>belt</u>.
- b When Julie arrived home, she looked <u>pale</u> and worried.
- c The <u>pale</u> winter sun provided little warmth.
- d A police car came <u>belting</u> round the corner with its siren on.
- e I don't think giving the TV a <u>belt</u> is going to make it work!
- f Unusually, she has dark skin and <u>pale</u> blue eyes.

3 Rewrite sentences a–f replacing the underlined words with one of the dictionary entries opposite.

Example When his car wouldn't start, he <u>hit</u> it.

When his car wouldn't start, he gave it a belt.

- a Drivers and passengers should <u>fasten their seatbelts</u> even for short journeys.
- b Just <u>shut up</u>! I can't hear myself think!
- c His salary <u>is nothing</u> in comparison with the amount of money his wife earns.
- d Some of the comedian's jokes were <u>completely unacceptable</u>.
- e The van was <u>tearing along</u> the motorway at 140 kph.
- f As the last song of the concert, the band <u>loudly performed</u> *America the Beautiful*.

Writing

Part 2 An informal email

1 Read the task below and Megan's reply. Underline eight words in Megan's email which are too formal and think of less formal alternatives.

> You have received an email from your English friend, Chloe. Read this part of the email and then write your email to Chloe.
>
> > Anyway, that's enough about me. What are your plans for the summer? Are you going to work at all? Any trips abroad planned? Please email and tell me.
> >
> > Take care
> >
> > Chloe

New Message

Send Chat Attach Address Fonts Colors Save As Draft

To:

Cc:

Subject:

Dear Chloe

Thanks so much for your email. It's great to hear from you! I finish my end-of-year examinations on 14th June, and then I'm on holiday for eight weeks! I can't wait! I'll really need a good rest, therefore I'm going to spend the first week doing absolutely nothing! Later in the summer, I'll be visiting my uncle, who resides in Italy, for a couple of weeks. I haven't got sufficient money for the plane ticket, but luckily my uncle has offered to purchase it for me. He's so generous! He'll be working while I'm there, so I'll have his house (and swimming pool) to myself! As soon as I get back from Italy, I'm going to look for employment. My brother will have left his job at the leisure centre to commence his university degree, so hopefully they'll be looking for somebody to replace him! Please write and tell me what your plans are for the summer. Are you going to visit that Spanish girl you encountered at Easter? Email again soon.

Lots of love

Megan

tip Emails can be formal or informal, depending on who is writing to whom. Use language appropriate to the context and do not mix formal and informal registers.

2 Read Megan's email again and say which of these activities she is planning to do during the summer holidays.

a buy some new clothes

b do nothing for a week

c do some schoolwork

d go abroad

e hang out with friends

f learn to surf

g look for a job

h take exams

3 Divide the main part of Megan's email into these four paragraphs.

a the immediate future

b a trip abroad

c getting a job

d questions for Chloe

4 Find a formal word in each of a–d and replace it with a less formal expression.

a All I have to do is assist with housework while I'm there.

b I've even informed my friends that I don't want to go out that week!

c You know, the one who resembles Penelope Cruz.

d I need to earn some funds before the next school year begins.

5 Decide where sentences a–d in 4 could go in Megan's email. (There is one per paragraph.)

6 Add phrases a–f to the language boxes. Which phrases are in the emails in 1?

a Keep in touch.

b Thanks so much for your …

c Love / Lots of love

d It was a nice surprise to get your …

e Take care.

f Email again soon.

●●● **Reacting** to the input

> Great to hear from you.

●●● **Finishing** an email

> Look forward to seeing you soon.

●●● **Signing** off

> Best wishes

7 Make a list of activities, real or imaginary, that you plan to do this summer. Try to think of three for each of these topics.

   a travel
   b sports and hobbies
   c work and study
   d time with friends

8 Make a paragraph plan. Choose the most interesting of the three ideas for each topic in 7. Then add notes to give more details of times, places, people, etc.

9 Imagine you received an email from an English-speaking friend, ending like Chloe's in 1. Read the **how to do it** box, then write your own answer in 140–190 words to the task in 1, using your plan from 8.

● **how** to do it

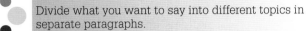

Begin by saying something about the email you have received.

Divide what you want to say into different topics in separate paragraphs.

Make sure you've included all the information required.

Check the number of words you have written.

tip Don't forget to read your work through carefully and check the spelling and grammar. You will lose marks if there are mistakes.

Review

1 Complete sentences a–f with the most appropriate adjective from 1–6.

1	bossy	4	argumentative
2	loyal	5	sensitive
3	sensible	6	easy-going

a Be careful what you say to Harry – he's quite _____ and gets upset very easily.

b You're always telling me what to do. I wish you weren't so _____ !

c Hannah is a very _____ friend – I know I can always rely on her to be there for me.

d Kelly is so _____ that she never really gets angry or upset about anything.

e Judy is very _____ – she'll ask somebody the time and then disagree with them.

f Think carefully before you make a decision. I know that you will, you're very _____ .

2 Correct any mistakes with the underlined verb forms in five of these sentences.

a Let's meet at the theatre tonight. The play <u>is starting</u> at 7.30.

b I'll probably be exhausted by the time I reach Edinburgh because <u>I'll have been driving</u> all morning.

c I can't go shopping with you tomorrow morning – <u>I'll have</u> my hair cut.

d By the time the next World Cup comes around, some of our most talented footballers <u>won't have played</u> any longer.

e <u>I'll be standing</u> here until you apologize for what you just said.

f <u>Will you have been leaving</u> by the time we get to the hotel?

3 Complete the sentences with the present or future simple of the verb in brackets.

a As soon as we _____ (arrive), we'll let you know.

b It's impossible to be sure, but I don't think she _____ (lose) her job.

c I _____ (be) amazed if Real Madrid don't win tonight's match.

d The doctors are keeping me in hospital until they _____ (know) what the problem is.

e The more money you spend now, the less you _____ (have) for your holiday next week.

f Do you think your brother _____ (help) us with our homework, if we ask him nicely?

4 Complete the text with the missing verbs.

Our RELATIONSHIPS **with our friends** 1 _____ **an important part in our lives, and help us to** 2 _____ **sense of the world. Megan has been a close friend of mine since primary school, and we're always together. In fact, some of our classmates** 3 _____ **fun of us, saying that we're like identical twins. Occasionally, we** 4 _____ **a row, but we never really fall out. The important thing is being able to** 5 _____ **sorry, if you know you are in the wrong.**

5 Rewrite each sentence a–d keeping the meaning the same. Use two to five words including the word given.

a Before we made a final decision, we considered everybody's opinion.
   account
   We _____ before making a final decision.

b Will you promise me that you won't tell anybody?
   word
   Will you _____ that you won't tell anybody?

c I contacted an old school friend after seeing his details on a website.
   touch
   Having seen an old school friend's details on a website, I _____ him.

d Only people who have participated in a triathlon can fully understand the excitement.
   part
   The only way to understand fully the excitement of a triathlon is _____ one.

Wild

Lead in

1 ▶4 **Listen to five people talking about where they live. For each one say if they**

- live in a city.
- live in the countryside.
- are happy with where they live.

2 ▶4 **Choose the correct word to complete each sentence a–g from the listening in 1. Then listen again and check.**

a The *sight/view* from my bedroom window is fantastic.
b I'm *right/very* in the middle of everything.
c The *scene/scenery* around here is amazing.
d I feel so *insulated/isolated* here.
e There are no *features/facilities* nearby.
f There's no sense of *community/society*.
g I love the peace and *quiet/quietness*.

3 Describe the photos and say how life would be different in each place. Use these adjectives to help you.

busy   cosmopolitan   crowded   isolated
noisy   peaceful   rural   urban

4 In pairs, take it in turns to describe where you live and what you like or dislike about it. Include words and phrases from 2 and 3 if possible.

Reading

Part 7 Multiple matching

1 Look at the photos. Using a dictionary if necessary, say which of the four animals shown

  a walks on all fours.

  b lives in a herd.

  c eats roots and nuts.

  d is a herbivore.

  e has hands with palms.

  f might help a shepherd.

2 You are going to read about four children who were raised by animals. Read the text quickly to find out

  a where each child was found.

  b how old each child was when they were found.

how to do it

Read the whole text once. If there are no section headings, it may help to add your own.

Read the questions. Answer any that you can immediately and underline the relevant parts of the text. You do not need to read these again.

Read each section of the text carefully, looking for answers to all the remaining questions.

3 Read the **how to do it** box. Then read the text again carefully, and for questions 1–10, choose from the children A–D. The children may be chosen more than once.

Which child

1 could run and jump very fast?

2 eventually returned to live in his family home?

3 hardly ever stood upright?

4 had unusual feet?

5 was not familiar with some common kinds of food?

6 did not go back to live with humans?

7 was very violent towards the people who captured him?

8 learned from animals how to look for things to eat?

9 was taken by a wild animal when very young?

10 copied the social rules and body language of the animals he lived with?

4 Find phrasal verbs a–f in the text and use the context to match them with their meanings (1–6).

a	bring up (l. 1)	1	find
b	come across (l. 6)	2	remove
c	come up to (l. 11)	3	take care of
d	take away (l. 31)	4	raise (a child)
e	keep up (l. 39)	5	approach
f	look after (l. 50)	6	go at the same speed

5 Use the ideas below to discuss what feral children might find difficult about rejoining society.

- eating and drinking
- games and playing
- family and friends
- school and education

BORN TO BE WILD

For centuries, people have told stories about children who were brought up by animals and became like animals themselves: so-called 'feral children'. *Tarzan of the Apes* and *The Jungle Book* are two famous fictional accounts. There are many other accounts which claim to be true, although it is sometimes difficult to separate fact from fantasy and folklore.

A In 1991, a Ugandan villager called Milly Sebba was searching for firewood when she came across a little boy with a group of five monkeys. She summoned help and the boy was captured and brought back to Milly's village. A villager identified the boy as John Ssebunya, last seen in 1988 at the age of two or three. Later, John claimed that he remembered monkeys coming up to him after a few days in the forest. They taught him, he says, to search for roots and nuts and to climb trees. Scientists are convinced that John is a genuine feral child. When left with a group of monkeys he avoids eye contact and approaches them from the side with open palms, just as monkeys do.

B Jean-Claude Auger, an anthropologist, was travelling across the Spanish Sahara in 1960 when he met some Nemadi nomads. They told him about a young boy who lived with a herd of gazelles. After searching for several days, Auger found the herd. The boy was about 10 years old and walked on all fours, only standing occasionally. One senior female seemed to act as his adoptive mother. He would eat roots with his teeth and appeared to be herbivorous. When Auger chased the boy in a jeep to see how fast he could run, he reached a speed of 50 kph, with leaps of about four metres. Unlike most of the feral children of whom there are records, the gazelle boy was never taken away from his wild companions.

C In July 1920 a leopard-boy was reported by EC Stuart Baker in the Journal of the Bombay Natural History Society. According to his report, the boy was stolen from his parents by a leopardess in the North Cachar Hills in India in about 1912, and three years later he was recovered and identified. At that time, the five-year-old ran on all fours so fast that an adult man could barely keep up. His hands and knees had hard skin on them and his toes were bent upright almost at right angles to his feet. When he was first caught, he bit and fought with everyone and would tear a chicken into pieces and eat it with astonishing speed, just like a wild animal.

D A feral child was found in Transylvania, Romania, in February 2002. One morning, shepherd Manolescu Ioan came upon a naked, wild-eyed child living in a cardboard box. Manolescu reported his find to the police, who later captured the boy. He had apparently lived alone in the forest for years, but doctors thought that he must have had some protection; perhaps he had been looked after by some of the many wild dogs in the region. He was the size of a normal four-year-old, but his missing front milk teeth suggested an actual age of seven. He ate whatever he was given, but didn't recognise fruit.

About a week after his capture, he was identified as Traian Caldarar, lost three years earlier at the age of four. After being re-educated at an orphanage, he was reunited with his mother, who lived in a remote village a few kilometres from where he had been found.

1

Vocabulary

Describing natural landscapes

1 Look at the photos. Say whether there are landscapes like these in your country and where, and in which other countries you might find them.

2 Identify one word which doesn't belong in each group a–e. Then explain the difference between the three words in the same group. Use a dictionary if necessary.

a	dune	mountain	hill	valley
b	lagoon	desert	lake	pond
c	field	forest	wood	jungle
d	beach	shore	coast	plain
e	bush	hedge	waterfall	tree

3 Match as many of the nouns in 2 as possible with the photos.

4 Imagine that you want to do the activities below with a friend from England. Say where in your country would be particularly good to do each one and why.

- mountain biking
- walking
- kayaking
- wind-surfing
- climbing

2

3

4

Grammar

Verb patterns GR p167

1 Read the first paragraph of the article opposite, which is about survival in the wilderness. Underline all the examples of infinitives (with and without *to*) and –*ing* forms, and circle the verbs which come immediately before them.

2 Put the verbs that you circled in 1 into Group A or B, depending on the verb pattern.
- Group A   verb + –*ing* form   *enjoy*
- Group B   verb + infinitive   *expect*

3 Complete gaps 1–12 in the article with the infinitive or –*ing* form of the verbs in brackets.

4 For each of 1–4, decide which sentence, a or b, makes most sense in the gap.

1 .... I'm sure he's very interesting.
   a I wish my neighbour would stop talking.
   b I wish my neighbour would stop to talk.
2 .... He therefore had no way of getting in touch with her.
   a He didn't remember to write down the woman's phone number.
   b He didn't remember writing down the woman's phone number.
3 .... However, the room still felt too hot.
   a He tried to open the window.
   b He tried opening the window.
4 William Faulkner began his career by writing short stories. ....
   a He went on to write novels.
   b He went on writing novels.

5 Complete these sentences in two different ways, once with an infinitive and once with an –*ing* form. Try to use a different verb each time.
   a When I leave school, I'll go on …
   b I wish people would stop …
   c I think I should try …
   d I'll always remember …

surviving in the wilderness

Many people enjoy travelling through wild and deserted landscapes, but few expect to end up in a genuine survival situation. The unexpected occasionally happens, however, so you should be prepared. Imagine finding yourself in the middle of a wilderness with a broken-down jeep and hardly any food and water. What should your priorities be? Should you stay with your vehicle and hope to be rescued? Or should you search for civilization and risk getting even more lost? Should you spend time searching for water or food first? Or should you postpone worrying about food and water until you have managed to find or build a shelter? If you are not sure, keep reading – this article could save your life!

Priority 1 shelter

Do not put off [1] .... (make) a shelter – it should be your first priority. Try [2] .... (enlarge) an existing, natural shelter, such as a hole in the ground below a fallen tree. If you happen [3] .... (be) near a rocky coast, build a shelter and cover it with wood from the beach. If you are on the move, stop [4] .... (build) your shelter while it is still light.

Priority 2 water

If you fail [5] .... (find) water, you will only survive for about three days (whereas you can survive for weeks without food). If there is no rain, try [6] .... (walk) through vegetation early in the morning to collect moisture in clothing. Avoid [7] .... (drink) water that looks or smells bad.

Priority 3 fire

Fire has many uses. It makes food more appetizing. If you can't face [8] .... (eat) raw worms, boil them in water to make a nourishing soup! Fire protects against dangerous animals, since many will not dare [9] .... (approach) it. And you can also use it for signalling to rescuers – before they give up [10] .... (look) for you!

Priority 4 food

It is quite easy to get food in the wild, if you know where to look. Many survival books suggest [11] .... (eat) a small amount of unknown plants to test if they are poisonous. However, we do not recommend [12] .... (do) this, since some plants are so poisonous that even a very small amount can cause serious health problems.

Listening

Part 2 Sentence completion

1 Read the paragraph below and explain in your own words what 'Wilderness Therapy' is.

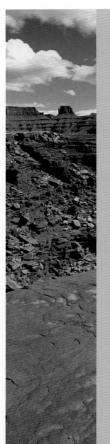

Wilderness Therapy

Redcliff Ascent is located in a remote area of desert and red rock in the state of Utah. It offers 'wilderness therapy' to troubled teenagers, 'helping them and their families find a new beginning'. Life there is not easy – it certainly isn't a holiday. During their stay, the students live a nomadic lifestyle, walking five to 10 kilometres each day from camp to camp. They have to build their own shelters for sleeping in, cook their own food and wash their own clothes: in short, to take full responsibility for their survival. They also learn how to work together in a group to solve problems. In the evenings, they sit round the fire and talk about their experiences. Education is an important part of RedCliff Ascent, and it focuses on seven key values: courage, self-discipline, respect, honesty, work ethic, trust and compassion.

courage
self-discipline
respect
honesty
work ethic
trust
compassion

2 ▶5 Listen once to the stories of two teenagers, Rachael and Ed, to find out who had the more positive experience at RedCliff Ascent.

3 ▶5 Listen again and complete sentences 1–10.
1 Many of the teenagers who go to RedCliff Ascent have broken the _____ .
2 The parents of many of the teenagers had no idea how to _____ their children.
3 At school, Rachael had been keen on long-distance _____ .
4 After returning from RedCliff, Rachael decided that she wanted to work with _____ .
5 Rachael continues to have a good relationship with her _____ .
6 Rachael's mother thinks that now Rachael looks really _____ .
7 Ed caused so many problems for his family that he had to find another _____ .
8 Ed's mother, Jane, thinks that Ed always wants more _____ .
9 Two weeks after the camp finished, Ed once again started _____ .
10 Ed's mother is hopeful that his second stay at RedCliff will be _____ .

4 Discuss why you think Wilderness Therapy is successful for many out-of-control teenagers.

Speaking

Part 2

1 Look at the photos. Say whether sentences a–f describe photo 1, photo 2 or both.

  a The people appear to be exploring a remote landscape.

  b The weather is bright and sunny.

  c There is a lot of dense vegetation.

  d They're higher than some of the clouds.

  e The ground is hard and rocky.

  f There are snow-capped mountains in the distance.

2 Describe what the people are doing and wearing by making a sentence about photo 1 or photo 2 using a–j.

  a jungle

  b mountain range

  c mountain bikes

  d on foot

  e in single file

  f side by side

  g long-sleeved jackets

  h short-sleeved T-shirts

  i spectacular scenery

  j dense vegetation

3 ▶6 Listen to five people talking about the photos. Say which photo each speaker is talking about and note down the words that give you the answers.

4 ▶6 Listen again and complete these phrases.

  a I think the people could be feeling quite _____ .

  b Personally, I would be _____ in their situation.

  c I _____ that they might be feeling quite tired.

  d I love that _____ of achievement you get from climbing up really high.

  e It looks as _____ they're quite bored.

  f I hate the _____ of not being able to see very far ahead.

  g They _____ be feeling excited.

  h They're _____ feeling a bit hot and sweaty.

5 Do this task.

> The photos show people enjoying themselves on holiday. Compare the photos and say why you think the people chose each particular type of holiday.

Use of English

Part 2 Open cloze

1 Phrases a and b can complete sentences 1–6 below, with similar meanings. Choose the correct preposition for each phrase, using a dictionary if necessary.

1 Many teenagers are .... Internet chat rooms.
   a addicted *on/to*   b hooked *on/to*

2 People who smoke are .... developing serious health problems.
   a *at/in* danger of   b *at/in* risk of

3 The streets in the town centre are .... litter.
   a full *of/with*   b covered *of/with*

4 Nobody knew .... his strange behaviour at the restaurant.
   a the reason *of/for*   b the cause *of/for*

5 The head teacher wanted to introduce school uniforms, but most of the teachers were not ....
   a *in/of* agreement   b *in/of* the same opinion

6 To be truly a great artist you cannot be .... failure.
   a frightened *with/of*   b worried *about/of*

> **tip** Prepositions are often difficult to use correctly because there are few rules. Try to learn them as part of longer phrases.

2 Choose the correct prepositions to complete a–i.

a My girlfriend arrived *at/to* the cinema ten minutes late.

b Whether progress is always a good thing depends *of/on* your point of view.

c People usually dress *in/with* colourful clothes at carnivals.

d The protests have had no effect *on/to* the government.

e Madonna was married *to/with* a film director.

f It took two weeks *for/of* my letter to arrive.

g The film *Titanic* is based *in/on* a true story.

h Australians are very good *at/in* many sports.

i Careless cyclists are in danger *with/of* getting injured.

3 Read the text quickly, ignoring the gaps, to find out why it isn't a good idea to keep wild animals as pets.

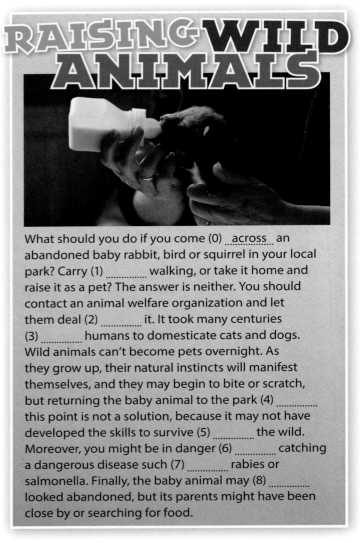

RAISING WILD ANIMALS

What should you do if you come (0) __across__ an abandoned baby rabbit, bird or squirrel in your local park? Carry (1) .... walking, or take it home and raise it as a pet? The answer is neither. You should contact an animal welfare organization and let them deal (2) .... it. It took many centuries (3) .... humans to domesticate cats and dogs. Wild animals can't become pets overnight. As they grow up, their natural instincts will manifest themselves, and they may begin to bite or scratch, but returning the baby animal to the park (4) .... this point is not a solution, because it may not have developed the skills to survive (5) .... the wild. Moreover, you might be in danger (6) .... catching a dangerous disease such (7) .... rabies or salmonella. Finally, the baby animal may (8) .... looked abandoned, but its parents might have been close by or searching for food.

4 Read the **how to do it** box. Then read the text again carefully and complete gaps 1–8 with one word each.

how to do it

Read the title and the text quickly for the general meaning. Don't fill in any gaps yet.

Read the text again, slowly, and try to fill in the missing words. Look at the words around the gap and try to work out what part of speech the missing word is.

Read the completed text to check your spelling and overall sense.

5 Discuss which animals make the best pets, and why.

Vocabulary

Collective nouns

1 Put these nouns into groups a–d according to their collective nouns.

bananas	birds	cards	dogs	cows
elephants	flowers	sheep		

a a flock of ....

b a herd of ....

c a pack of ....

d a bunch of ....

2 Match nouns a–h with the groups of people they describe (1–8).

a audience 1 people acting in a play or film

b cast 2 people who play sport together, or work together

c crew 3 people working in an organization

d crowd 4 people watching a film, concert, play, etc.

e gang 5 a group of experts

f panel 6 a large group of people

g staff 7 people working on a ship or a plane

h team 8 a group of people who may cause trouble

3 Complete these sentences with collective nouns from 1 and 2.

a Apparently a fight broke out last night between two .... of football fans.

b As we ate our lunch in the park, a .... of pigeons circled round and landed next to us.

c We had to stop the car when we came across a farmer driving a .... of cows down the lane.

d Hospital .... have threatened to go on strike unless they receive a pay rise.

e The .... of the show includes some big Hollywood stars.

f I always send my girlfriend a .... of roses on Valentine's Day.

g A .... gathered outside the cinema, hoping to see the stars at the film premiere.

h The .... sat spellbound throughout the entire concert.

Writing

Part 1 An essay

1 **Read the exam task below. Are these sentences true or false?**

  a You must include your own opinion in the essay.

  b You can choose which of the three notes you wish to write about.

  c You don't have to give reasons for your opinion.

In your English class you have been talking about the advantages and disadvantages of allowing cars free access to city centres. Now your English teacher has asked you to write an essay. Write an essay using *all* the notes and give reasons for your point of view.

> **Essay question**
> Cars should be banned from town and city centres. Do you agree?
>
> **Notes**
> Things to write about
> 1 pollution
> 2 public transport
> 3 your own idea

tip Aim to use grammatically correct sentences with accurate spelling and punctuation in a style appropriate for the situation.

2 **Read the model essay. Answer the questions.**

  a What is the writer's own idea in the fourth paragraph? Choose from:
accidents   freedom to travel   safety   shopping

  b What is the writer's own point of view?

In recent years, cars have been banned from towns and cities in a number of countries. However, I am not convinced that the bans are always justified.

I agree that it may be wise to ban cars if there is a serious problem with pollution. However, I don't think air pollution is very bad in most towns and cities, so to my mind an outright ban is not justified from that point of view.

If cars were banned from town centres, we would have to rely on public transport. However, public transport is poor in many places, so even short journeys could become difficult and inconvenient. Furthermore, elderly and disabled people find buses and trams difficult to use and rely on their cars to get around.

In my opinion, we should be free to travel anywhere we like in our cars. Cars make life much easier and better for most people, so we should not restrict their use.

In conclusion, I firmly believe that it would be wrong to ban all cars from city centres without a very good reason, for example a serious problem with air pollution.

3 Complete the table with these words. Then find four of them in the essay.

clear	firmly	furthermore
mind	only	opinion	see

expressing opinions

in my ....   to my ....

as I .... it   I .... believe

making additional points

....   moreover

not .... that   it's also .... that

4 Read the exam task. Add a third idea of your own.

Essay question
It is better to live in the city than the country. Do you agree?

Notes
Things to write about
1 things to do in your spare time
2 which is better for your health
3 your own idea

how to do it

Read the task carefully.

Using the notes, brainstorm ideas for and against the proposition in the essay title.

Decide if you agree or disagree with the proposition.

5 Read the **how to do it box**. Develop the ideas in the notes below the essay question. Complete the chart below.

1 things to do in your spare time	
in the countryside	in the city
2 which is better for your health	
the countryside	the city
3 your own idea	
the countryside	the city

6 Write your essay in 140–190 words in an appropriate style. Use your notes from 5.

tip In the exam you have to write two essays of 140–190 words in 80 minutes. You should plan what you are going to write, but don't take too long doing this. Spend a maximum of 5 to 10 minutes on your plan.

Review

1 For a–e form words from the letters in brackets to complete the sentences.

a The _____ (lawratfel) plunged 100 metres into the _____ (lavyel) below.

b To reach the lost city, the explorers had to swim across a wide _____ (noolag) and cut through thick _____ (lenjug).

c Although the _____ (toasc) is very beautiful, there are few _____ (scebaeh) where you can swim safely.

d Golden _____ (nesud) stretched for miles across the _____ (steder).

e There's a small _____ (nodp) in our garden, surrounded by _____ (seshub).

2 Complete sentences a–h with the infinitive or *–ing* form of these words, as appropriate.

arrive   eat   go   relax   smoke   see   study   walk

a My grandfather found it very difficult to give up _____ after forty years.

b Most people enjoy _____ at home at the weekend.

c After he finishes school, my brother hopes _____ history at university.

d She put off _____ the dentist, even though she had toothache.

e I'd suggest _____ to Portugal in the spring, before it gets too hot.

f I can't face _____ any breakfast before 8 o'clock in the morning.

g He called the police, but they failed _____ before the burglar had escaped.

h You should avoid _____ through Central Park alone at night.

3 Choose the correct form of the verb to complete each of these sentences.

a He left school at the age of 18 and went on *to do/ doing* a degree at Cambridge.

b They started playing tennis after lunch and went on *to play/playing* until it was nearly dark.

c Nobody answered the door when he knocked, so he tried *to tap/tapping* on the window.

d She tried *to move/moving* the bed but couldn't, because it was too heavy.

e He walked halfway down the street and then stopped *to tie/tying* his shoes.

f Would you please stop *to talk/talking* and listen!

4 Complete gaps 1–5 in the text with the correct prepositions.

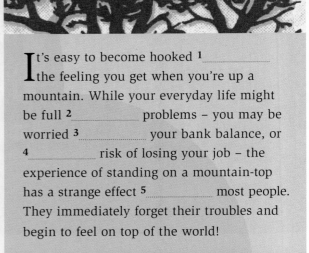

It's easy to become hooked **1** _____ the feeling you get when you're up a mountain. While your everyday life might be full **2** _____ problems – you may be worried **3** _____ your bank balance, or **4** _____ risk of losing your job – the experience of standing on a mountain-top has a strange effect **5** _____ most people. They immediately forget their troubles and begin to feel on top of the world!

What's so funny?

Lead in

1 Put these words into two groups, **a** and **b**, depending on their meaning.
Which word belongs in both groups? Check your answers in a dictionary.

a something that makes you laugh
b something out of the ordinary

amusing	bizarre	mysterious	comical	funny	unusual	hilarious
peculiar	odd	humorous	hysterical	strange	weird	

2 In pairs, talk about the following.

a a film or TV programme that you find hilarious
b a TV personality who is humorous
c something strange that has happened to you
d something unusual that you own
e a mysterious place that you've heard of
f an odd fact that you know

3 Describe the photos below. Which do you think is the funniest? Which is the cleverest? Why?

Reading

Part 6 Gapped text

1 Look at the photos. What unusual abilities do you think these people have? Discuss your ideas in pairs.

2 Read the text below quickly and check your ideas from 1. What other special abilities are mentioned?

STRANGE BUT TRUE

Characters with superhuman abilities are common in comic books and films, but are usually confined to the world of fantasy. Very occasionally, however, similar powers
5 can be found in real people. Remember Magneto in *X-Men*? Well, meet 'Mister Magnet', a retired builder from Malaysia who now has a new career as an entertainer. (1) .... There were no
10 hooks or other fasteners; it remained stuck to his body purely by means of some strange force. Mr Liew Thow Lin discovered his bizarre ability after reading a magazine article about a family in Taiwan with the same gift.
15 (2) .... Scientists have investigated Mr Lin and believe that he does indeed have the ability he claims to have. Rather than magnetism, however, the effect is due to suction, and works like the suckers on
20 an octopus's tentacles.

Gustav Graves, the villain in the James Bond film *Die Another Day*, has plenty of time for making evil plans because, unlike normal people, he does not need to sleep. Hai Ngoc, a sixty-four-year-old farmer
25 from Vietnam, claims that he has not slept since he became ill with a fever in 1973. He doesn't use the additional waking hours for evil plans, though. (3) .... In one three-month period, he used the night-times to dig two large fish ponds.
30 Amazingly, thousands and thousands of sleepless nights have not damaged his health, it seems. (4) .... However, perhaps not surprisingly, he has admitted to feeling a little grumpy.

Everybody knows that Superman uses X-rays to see
35 through walls. While this would be impossible for a real person to do, there have been very rare cases of humans developing alternative forms of sight. Ben Underwood, for example, became completely blind at the age of three, but that didn't stop him from getting around. He
40 didn't use a guide dog, a stick or even his hands to feel

tip Look for grammar and vocabulary links before and after each gap and in A–G.

3 Read the text again carefully and the **tip** box. Then complete gaps 1–6 with sentences A–G, using the underlined words to help you. There is one extra sentence.

A <u>The answer</u> is simple but remarkable: he learned to use sound.

B In fact, he is physically strong and medical tests have discovered no serious problems.

C That's why he kept his amazing ability a secret, even from his family.

D <u>Curious</u>, he took several heavy metal objects and placed them against his skin; they all stuck to him and didn't fall to the floor.

E <u>On the contrary</u>, he puts them to good use, doing extra work or guarding his property against thieves.

F However, it wasn't until he reached the age of sixteen that he began performing publicly.

G Recently, he attracted international attention by pulling a car which was chained to a metal plate on his skin.

4 Explain how the underlined words in A–G helped you to match the sentences with the gaps. Which other words helped you do the task?

5 Discuss which of the special abilities from the text is

a the weirdest

b the most useful

c the least useful

6 Imagine you could have any superpower you can think of. What would you choose and how would you use it?

his way. So how did he navigate? (5) .... In the same way that bats use echoes to find their way around in the darkness, Ben developed his own form of sonar. He would make short clicks with his tongue and by listening to
45 the echoes, he could locate objects around him. Ben amazed scientists and doctors with his ability to get around – by bicycle as well as on foot – in spite of his total blindness.

Monsters in comic books may grab aeroplanes out of the sky, but they rarely eat them. Unlike Michel Lotito, a
50 Frenchman who lived between 1950 and 2007. He had the ability to eat all kinds of materials that most people would find completely indigestible: metal, glass, rubber, plastic, and so on. His bizarre eating habits began when he was a child. (6) .... He once ate an aeroplane –
55 a Cessna 150 – which he broke up and swallowed piece by piece over two years. Apparently, the walls of his intestines were twice as thick as most people's, and he had extra-powerful stomach acids which helped him digest some of the metal.

Vocabulary

Extreme adjectives

1 Match adjectives a–l with their extreme forms below.

> ancient   astounded   boiling   exhausted
> filthy   freezing   furious   gorgeous
> hideous   hilarious   spotless   starving

a	attractive	g	surprised
b	ugly	h	funny
c	dirty	i	angry
d	clean	j	tired
e	hot	k	old
f	cold	l	hungry

2 Work in pairs to find as many extreme adjectives as possible for a–d.

a   very big
b   very small
c   very good
d   very bad

3 Decide which of the words in a–e correctly completes each sentence.

a   The cooker was *a bit/very/totally* spotless when Steve had finished cleaning it.

b   Kate missed her appointment because her train was *extremely/totally/utterly* late.

c   Put your hat and scarf on. It's *absolutely/extremely/very* freezing out there.

d   Josh was feeling *quite/totally/absolutely* tired by the time he got home from work.

e   I'm *completely/utterly/very* sorry, but I've forgotten your name.

Grammar

Talking about the past
GR p166–167

1 Choose the correct tense to complete a–h. Explain your choice, using the Grammar Reference section if necessary.

a   *I've done/I've been doing* the ironing. I've only got three more shirts to do.

b   When I phoned Karen, she was worried because her brother *didn't arrive/hadn't arrived* home.

c   I've never tried Vietnamese food, but *I had/I've had* Thai.

d   I *found/was finding* a wallet when I was walking home from the shops.

e   Harry was sweating by the time he arrived at the cinema because he *had been/was* running.

f   Have you ever *ridden/been riding* a horse?

g   By the time we found the restaurant, it *closed/had closed*.

h   At the time of the accident, George *wasn't wearing/didn't wear* a seatbelt.

2 Correct the mistakes in sentences a–h.

a   I've never been believing in Santa Claus.

b   I've been asking him three times, but he hasn't told me yet.

c   Rita and Ahmed have arrived two minutes ago.

d   By the time the fire brigade arrived, the fire had burnt for over an hour.

e   How long have you studied Chinese?

f   According to the police, the thieves have left the country a few hours after committing the crime.

g   How often have you been travelling by plane?

h   My aunt isn't here yet, but my uncle has arrived last night.

3 Complete sentences a–h with your own ideas, using an appropriate tense.

a I've never tried bungee jumping, but ....
b Julie's hair was wet because ....
c As they were getting onto the train, ...
d By the time we arrived at the shop, ...
e I .... since 8 o'clock this morning.
f She .... three times this year.
g He opened the door, ran outside and ....
h At midnight last night, George ....

4 Complete the text with an appropriate form of the verbs in brackets. Sometimes more than one tense is possible.

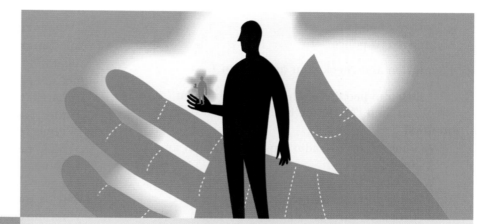

By the time I *arrived* (arrived) at the wedding, many of the guests
¹ .... (go) home. Monica ² .... (sit) on the stairs, red-eyed. She
³ .... (cry), but she was OK now. 'I ⁴ .... (wait) for a taxi since
ten o'clock,' she explained. 'I ⁵ .... (phone) three times, but it ⁶ ....
(not come).' I ⁷ .... (offer) her a lift home and she ⁸ .... (accept).
As we ⁹ .... (walk) to my car, she ¹⁰ .... (touch) my hand gently.
'I ¹¹ .... (think) about you a lot recently,' she said. 'You're one of the
kindest people I ¹² .... (meet) in my life.'

5 Continue the story in 4 with your own ideas. Start with the words 'At that moment, …' and end with 'we both laughed'. Write 60–80 words.

Listening

Part 1 Multiple choice

1 **Read questions 1–8 in 3 below. Try to match each situation with these pairs of words. Compare your answers with a partner.**

   a training   mental
   b coach   backpacks
   c analyse   giggle
   d view   armchair
   e symptom   region
   f property   apartment
   g sorry   hang on
   h arrested   police

2 ▶7 **Listen and check your answers to 1.**

3 ▶7 **Listen to people talking in eight different situations, and choose the best answer for each question.**

   1 You hear part of a radio programme about an epidemic.
     Who was affected by it?
     A some children and teachers
     B people in various schools and villages
     C three schoolgirls and everyone in their villages

   2 You hear a woman complaining about her hotel room.
     What is she most unhappy about?
     A the location of the room
     B the equipment in the room
     C the furniture in the room

   3 You hear a man being interviewed about a world record attempt.
     How is he feeling?
     A confident and determined
     B well-prepared and relaxed
     C surprised and nervous

   4 You hear a woman talking to a friend.
     Why is she talking to him?
     A to arrange to meet later
     B to give him encouragement
     C to apologize for her behaviour

   5 You hear a man talking about a recent holiday.
     How did he feel about sleeping in the jungle?
     A It was frightening but interesting.
     B It was exciting but uncomfortable.
     C It was tiring and too hot.

   6 You hear a man talking.
     What is his job?
     A an estate agent
     B a builder
     C an architect

   7 You hear a report about a scientific study.
     What did the study show?
     A Each person produces only one type of laughter.
     B Men and women tend to produce different types of laughter.
     C Men and women usually laugh at different things.

   8 You hear a news item on the radio.
     What is the item about?
     A an intruder at the Prime Minister's residence
     B improved security at the Prime Minister's residence
     C an injury to a detective during an arrest

Speaking

Parts 3 and 4

1 Describe each of the photos. What different sorts of shows and exhibitions are they?

2 ▶8 Listen to two people arranging to go out. Number the photos in the order you hear them mentioned. How many other shows do they talk about? What do they decide to book tickets for?

3 ▶8 Listen again and say which of these phrases for making suggestions you hear.

a Let's go to …
b Well, why don't we go to…?
c How does this sound?
d Shall we go and see …?
e How about …?
f I know. What about … ?
g I've got an idea. We could …
h Do you fancy going to see …?
i Would you like to … ?

4 Choose the correct words in italics to complete these opinions.

a I don't *think/find* modern dance very interesting.
b It's *described/supposed* to be brilliant.
c I'm not really *on/into* photography.
d In *fact/effect*, I really don't like sculpture at all.
e To be *honest/true*, modern fashion just makes me laugh.
f Pop music isn't really my *thing/business*.
g I'm not a *strong/big* fan of novelty acts.

5 Read the **how to do it** box. Then in pairs, look at the diagram and do the tasks below. Use phrases from 3 and 4.

Imagine you are going out for the evening. Here are some of the places you could go. Talk to each other about what you would find interesting or uninteresting about these different forms of entertainment.

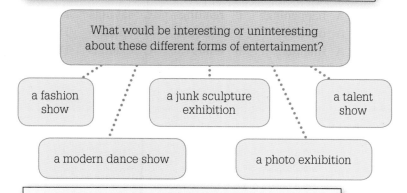

What would be interesting or uninteresting about these different forms of entertainment?

a fashion show
a junk sculpture exhibition
a talent show
a modern dance show
a photo exhibition

Decide which one you are going to book tickets for.

6 Discuss these Part 4 questions.

a Do you think there is a good variety of shows and exhibitions to go to in your area? What additional shows would improve the choice?

b Is it ever worth going to see a show or exhibition that doesn't sound very interesting? Why/Why not?

c Some people think fashion shows are a waste of time and money. Do you agree? Explain your answer.

d Is it important to like the same kinds of entertainment as your close friends? Why/Why not?

how to do it

Give your own opinions clearly and simply.
Listen to your partner and react to what they say.
Try to correct any mistakes you make, but don't spend time worrying about them.
Keep talking until the examiner stops you.

Use of English

Part 1 Multiple-choice cloze

1 Discuss which of the adjectives below you would use to describe yourself and any brothers and sisters you have.

> adventurous creative humorous
> rebellious risk-taking unconventional

2 Read the newspaper report opposite ignoring the gaps, and choose the best heading (a, b or c).

a Older siblings are more competitive.

b Younger siblings have fewer skills.

c Younger siblings are more humorous.

3 Read the the **tip** box. Then read the text again carefully and decide which answer (A, B, C or D) best fits each gap.

> **C**hildren with older brothers and sisters find it easier to (0) _make_ people laugh, a survey has suggested. Just over half of younger siblings who (1) .... part in the study said it was easy to be humorous, compared with a third of those who were (2) .... 'Younger siblings have to compete (3) .... parental attention, so they are often risk-taking, and also more humorous,' said psychologist Richard Wiseman, who carried out the study. 'On the other (4) .... , older children frequently take on more serious roles, while children without siblings don't feel the (5) .... to compete at all.'
>
> These (6) .... tie in with other research on family position and personality. Wiseman said that University of California research had suggested that, because younger children had not had the chance to (7) .... the same skills and abilities as their older siblings, they had to find novel ways of gaining attention. This (8) .... to make them more creative, unconventional, adventurous and rebellious.

tip Try to think of possible answers before looking at the options.

0	A force	B push	C make	D encourage
1	A had	B took	C did	D played
2	A firstborn	B major	C primary	D newborn
3	A over	B on	C in	D for
4	A hand	B side	C way	D matter
5	A want	B idea	C need	D lack
6	A happenings	B readings	C sayings	D findings
7	A develop	B increase	C enlarge	D grow
8	A intends	B tends	C extends	D sends

Vocabulary

Phrasal verbs with *put*

1 Complete sentences a–h with *up* or *down*.

a I must find a new apartment. I can't put *up with/down with* my noisy neighbours any longer!

b It's not surprising she lacks confidence. Her older siblings are always putting her *up/down*.

c I couldn't find a hotel room, so my friend agreed to put me *up/down* for the night.

d He was finding it difficult to sleep at night. At first, he put this *up to/down to* stress.

e Armed rebels tried to overthrow the government, but the army soon put *up/down* the revolt.

f I need several thousand euros to pay for a year abroad before university. Fortunately, my parents have agreed to put *up/down* half the amount.

g Because of a shortage of oil and gas, energy companies have put *up/down* their prices.

h He admitted vandalizing the bus stop, but claimed his friends had put him *up to/down to* it.

2 Rewrite the sentences in 1 using the verbs below in an appropriate form instead of phrasal verbs. Use a dictionary to help you, if necessary.

> accommodate   suppress   explain   humiliate
> increase   persuade   provide   tolerate

3 In pairs, think of as many other phrasal verbs with *put* as you can. Then check in your dictionary.

4 Complete sentences a–h with phrasal verbs with *put*.

a To be a good musician, you need to put _____ hours of practice.

b He's terrible at explaining things. He finds it impossible to put _____ his points clearly.

c These forest fires have been burning for days, despite all the efforts to put them _____ .

d Is he really upset – or is he just putting it _____ ?

e I still love her, despite everything that she's put me _____ .

f The government has put _____ a new plan to improve the transport system.

g She's really messy. She never puts anything _____ in its proper place.

h I'd like to travel more, but all those delays at airports really put me _____ .

5 In pairs, talk about a–c.

a things you've learned to do by putting in a lot of time

b things that would put you off being friends with someone

c things you don't enjoy but have to put up with

Writing

Part 2 An article

1 Read the task and the article. Is the style formal, informal or neutral? Give evidence to support your opinion.

> You have seen the following announcement in an international magazine for schools. Write an article of 140–190 words in an appropriate style.
>
> **Competition!**
>
> Write an article about the funniest person you know. It could be someone you know personally or a famous person. We will publish the best articles in next month's edition.

A very funny person

If you bumped into my granddad, you probably wouldn't imagine he was particularly funny, but he has a great sense of humour and is the funniest person I know.

He's always telling jokes. He knows loads of good ones – goodness knows how he manages to remember them all! He also loves telling us stories from his youth which always have an amusing ending. For example, he said he once fell asleep on a bus journey. When he woke up, it was dark and the bus was back at the bus station. The driver had disappeared and the doors were locked. He had to spend the whole night on the bus!

He also loves playing practical jokes on people, but the jokes are always harmless. He once bought some fake spiders from a joke shop and hung them from the light in the dining room. You should have seen my mum's face when she spotted them!

So, as you can see, there's never a dull moment when my granddad's around. He's like a big kid, and that's what makes him such good company!

2 Read the **how to do it** box. Has the writer followed all of the advice?

how to do it

- Think of a good title for your article that will attract the readers' attention.
- Divide your article into clearly organized paragraphs.
- Give your opinion, reaction or final summarizing comment in the final paragraph.
- Think about who will be reading the article and adopt an appropriate style (it could be formal or informal).

3 Find informal words or phrases in the article that mean:

a   met by chance

b   a lot of

c   present in a place; there

d   child

4 Read the task in 1 and plan your article. Make notes in the chart.

Who are you going to write about?
First example of why he/she is funny
Second example of why he/she is funny

5 Write your article.

Review

1 Rewrite the text using extreme adjectives to replace the underlined phrases.

> Juliet sat on the edge of her bed. She looked at her bedroom floor. It was <u>very dirty</u>. She wanted to clean her room. She normally kept it <u>very clean</u>. But she felt <u>very tired</u>. Then she got a text message. She was <u>very surprised</u> when she read it. It was from Liam, the <u>very attractive</u> boy in her class. The message said: 'Fancy lunch? I'm <u>very hungry</u>.' Suddenly, Juliet felt more optimistic. 'Perhaps this isn't going to be a <u>very bad</u> day after all,' she thought, and gave a <u>very small</u> smile.

2 Choose the best word, a or b, to complete 1–5.

1 My aunt keeps her house .... spotless.
   a extremely   b totally

2 You should bring a jumper. It's .... freezing outside.
   a absolutely   b completely

3 We were .... sorry to hear about your accident.
   a very   b utterly

4 The train was .... late and we missed the start of the play.
   a utterly   b extremely

5 Harry was .... tired by the end of the race.
   a totally   b quite

3 Correct the phrasal verbs in a–h.

a The heat doesn't put me on going to Africa.

b Don't criticize me! You're always putting me through.

c I can't afford to shop there any more. They've put forward their prices.

d Put in your mobile until the lesson has finished!

e When he speaks French, he finds it hard to put out what he's trying to say.

f I wasn't really miserable. I was just putting it out.

g You'll pass the exam if you put away enough hours of revision.

h If you ever visit London, don't book a hotel room – we'll put you away for the night.

4 Read the text below and decide which answer (A, B, C or D) best fits each gap 1–8.

Can the use of humour in online courses (0) _produce_ good results for students? Psychology professors Mark Shatz and Frank LoShiavo think so. 'Students often (1) .... online courses as boring and impersonal, (2) .... we decided to introduce humour into our teaching in the form of jokes and cartoons,' said Shatz. Forty-four students did (3) .... the original course or the more humorous course. The professors then counted the number of times that students (4) .... part in online discussions, and asked students how much they enjoyed the course overall. The students who did the more humorous course were more (5) .... to join in discussions and also seemed to enjoy the course more. 'Teachers don't need to be comedians,' said Shatz. 'Our job is not to (6) .... students laugh. Our job is to (7) .... them learn and if humour makes learning more fun, then everyone benefits.' On the other (8) ...., humour can sometimes be a barrier to learning. 'If I make my students laugh too much, they'll remember my funny story and not what I am teaching them,' admitted Shatz.

0	A propose	B present	C produce	D prepare
1	A believe	B view	C think	D look
2	A that	B as	C so	D then
3	A either	B both	C nor	D each
4	A had	B took	C played	D did
5	A probable	B possible	C expected	D likely
6	A force	B cause	C make	D create
7	A assist	B help	C teach	D get
8	A side	B way	C matter	D hand

Inspired

Lead in

1 Look at the photos and answer these questions about each person.

   a What different talents do they need?

   b Where might they get their inspiration from?

   c What kind of hard work do they
      each have to put in?

   d Who do you think has to
      work hardest to be successful?

   e Who do you admire most?

2 Using the ideas below, discuss which of the
people shown you'd most like to be and why.

> become famous
> make money
> work alone
> create something beautiful
> change the world
> travel the world

3 In pairs, think of as many other professions
as you can that require inspiration.

singer-songwriter

author

inventor/scientist

film director

Reading

Part 6 Gapped text

1 Read the magazine article about songwriting quickly. Which musician:

  a   says that self-criticism is important?

  b   often finds inspiration in other people's music?

  c   spends a lot of time alone?

  d   can easily get distracted by electronic gadgets?

2 Read the article again carefully, then choose from the sentences A–G the one that fits each gap (1–6). There is one extra sentence which you do not need to use.

  A   It is so easy to let your life get filled up with other stuff – cooking, cleaning, going to the bank, looking after your baby.

  B   That can happen occasionally: sometimes, I'm walking down the street and I suddenly hear a fragment of music that I can later work into a song.

  C   Now that I'm a songwriter myself, I find watching other musicians can be frustrating.

  D   If you get stuck, take a break and do something else.

  E   When you're writing, you have to be very disciplined, to the point of being awkward: turn off your phone and find a space to work where you won't be distracted.

  F   Then I pace around the room, or go and get a snack.

  G   In fact, if I am feeling down, the last thing I want to do is write; though it's important sometimes just to sit down and get on with it, however you're feeling.

WHEN THE MUSIC TAKES YOU

What do artists go through when they create? *The Guardian* newspaper asked leading songwriters Fyfe Dangerfield of the band Guillemots and Canadian–American singer-songwriter Martha Wainwright how they find inspiration.

Fyfe Dangerfield One of the most difficult things about writing music is the sheer number of distractions: mobiles, email, Twitter, YouTube. **1** ☐

I used to think that being inspired was about sitting around waiting for ideas to come to you. **2** ☐ But generally, it's not like that at all. I liken the process to seeing ghosts: the ideas are always there, half-formed. It's about being in the right state of mind to take them and turn them into something that works.

For me, the image of the tortured artist is a myth. You don't need to be miserable to write songs. **3** ☐ Your creativity is like a tap: if you don't use it, it gets clogged up.

We all have that small voice that tells us we're rubbish, and we need to learn when to silence it. But when it comes to recording or mixing, you do need to be your own critic and editor. It's a bit like having children: you don't interfere with the birth, but as your child grows up, you don't let it run wild.

Martha Wainwright I definitely don't have rules – I'm pretty disorganized. In fact, I often have to force myself to stop doing domestic chores and sit down to write. **4** ☐ These everyday things do come through in my songwriting, though. Most of my songs are defined by a sense of loneliness, of isolation, that I probably get from spending a lot of time on my own.

The little images that I get from sitting alone in my apartment – the way the light is falling through the window; the man I just saw walk by on the other side of the street – find their way into snatches of lyrics. I write in short spurts – for five, 10, 15 minutes. **5** ☐

When I first moved to New York some years ago, I used to go to concerts every night – I would see six or seven performances a week. **6** ☐ I want to be the one up there performing. But every so often I see someone who inspires me to try something different. That happened recently with Sufjan Stevens. I saw him perform in Prospect Park, and his sound was so huge and poppy that I went home thinking: 'I should really try something like that.'

3 Match the phrasal verbs with the meanings, using the text to help you.

a sit around (l.11)
b turn into (l.15)
c turn off (sentence E)
d get on with (sentence G)
e look after (sentence A)
f fill up (sentence A)

1 stop the flow of power to a machine or device
2 care for
3 continue doing something, especially after an interruption
4 spend time sitting down, doing very little
5 make full
6 make something become something else

4 Read the dictionary entry for ***think up***. How does the entry indicate that it is a separable phrasal verb?

> **ˌthink sth↔ˈup** 🔑 (*informal*) to create sth in your mind **SYN** **devise, invent**: *Can't you think up a better excuse than that?*

Oxford Advanced Learner's Dictionary, 8th edition

5 Decide which other verbs in 3 take an object, then check in your dictionary to see if they are separable or not.

Vocabulary

Films

1 Look at the list of film types below and think of one example of each type.

a	action	h	historical drama
b	adventure	i	musical
c	animation	j	romantic comedy
d	comedy	k	science-fiction
e	crime	l	war
f	disaster	m	western
g	horror		

2 Label the adjectives below as a, b or c. Some may fit into more than one category.

a positive   b negative   c neutral

boring	gripping	scary
funny	powerful	terrible
moving	slow	violent
serious		

3 Say which adjectives in 2 you generally associate with the film types in 1.

4 Tell a partner about a film you really liked, and one you didn't like at all. Say what you liked or didn't like about each one using these words.

acting	costumes	ending
locations	music	special effects
plot	stunts	

Grammar

Simple and continuous tenses
GR p163–164

1 Name the tenses in italics in a–k and choose the correct one to complete each sentence.

a Yesterday evening, we *were having/had* dinner and watched a film on television.

b I don't usually like desserts, but this ice-cream *is tasting/tastes* wonderful.

c The sun *was rising/rose* by the time they finally got to bed.

d Our team *are playing/play* well, but the score is still 0–0.

e Your face is red. *Have you been sitting/Have you sat* in the sun?

f Since his first film in 1984, Johnny Depp *has been playing/has played* many different roles.

g This time next week, I*'ll be sitting/sit* on a beach in the Caribbean.

h It's a good story, but I*'m not believing/don't believe* that it's true!

i Can we stop for a while? We*'ve been walking/'ve walked* since 10 o'clock this morning!

j If you don't study hard for these exams, you*'ll be regretting/'ll regret* it.

k I *always leave/'m always leaving* my keys at home. I'm so forgetful.

2 Read quotations a–e and correct any continuous forms which should be simple forms, as in the example.

Example   'I'm thinking I'm thinking *I think* a pillow should be the peace symbol, not the dove. The pillow has more feathers than the dove, and it isn't having *doesn't have* a beak to peck you with.'

a Everywhere is within walking distance if you're having the time.

b I'm remembering when the candle shop burned down. Everyone was standing around singing 'Happy Birthday'.

c I've had a poor memory for as long as I'm remembering.

d I bought a new Japanese car. When I turn on the radio, I'm not understanding a word they're saying.

e There are two types of people in this world, good and bad. The good are sleeping better, but the bad are seeming to enjoy the waking hours much more.

3 Compare these pairs of sentences and explain the difference in meaning between the verbs in italic.

a I *don't see* why you can't help me with my homework.

They *aren't seeing* each other – they're just good friends.

b What *do you think* of Tarantino's latest film?

We*'re thinking* of going to the cinema tomorrow night.

c Our teacher *feels* that we're working harder this year.

We*'re feeling* optimistic about the exam.

d You smile a lot when you *have* a baby.

You don't smile much when you*'re having* a baby.

4 Complete the dialogue by putting the verbs in brackets into the correct tense (future, present or present perfect, simple or continuous).

Joanna You _____ ¹ (sit) on that sofa since lunchtime. What _____ you _____ ² (do)?

Wesley A crossword.

Joanna You _____ ³ (always do) crosswords!

Wesley Well, I _____ ⁴ (enjoy) them. Anyway, I _____ ⁵ (finish) it soon, if you _____ ⁶ (let) me concentrate!

Joanna I _____ ⁷ (never like) crosswords.

Wesley Sshhh! I _____ ⁸ (think)! Four across, 'get better' …

Joanna 'Improve'. Seems pretty easy to me.

Wesley They aren't all that easy. I _____ ⁹ (have) trouble with some of them. For example, can you think of a word that _____ ¹⁰ (mean) 'magnificent'?

Joanna 'Wonderful'?

Wesley No, it _____ ¹¹ (not fit). Eight letters.

Joanna Oh, I _____ ¹² (know). It's 'splendid'.

Wesley What about this one – a small insect that _____ ¹³ (bite)?

Joanna A mosquito?

Wesley That's it! I _____ ¹⁴ (do) it!

5 Complete questions a–e with an appropriate verb and tense (simple or continuous). Then discuss the questions in pairs.

a What _____ you _____ this evening?

b How long _____ you _____ English?

c What _____ you usually _____ on Saturday evenings?

d Where do you think you _____ in ten years' time?

e What _____ you _____ when the teacher came into the room?

Listening

Part 1 Multiple choice

how to do it

Read the questions and options carefully before you listen. Decide what kind of information you are listening for.

In the exam the eight situations are unconnected. Focus on each one in turn. Mark your answer after the first listening, then check it during the second listening. If you aren't sure, make a guess.

1 ▶9 Read the **how to do it** box and the example question below, including the three options. Then listen and mark your answer. Say which words helped you decide.

Example You hear two people in a hospital.
Where must the woman's bag be?
A in the cafeteria
B by the lifts
C in the chemist's

2 ▶10 Listen to people talking in eight different situations and choose the best answers.

1 You hear two friends discussing homework.
How does Emma feel about maths lessons?
A She thinks maths is more important than art.
B She doesn't think the teacher explains very well.
C She wishes she didn't have to do maths.

2 You hear a woman talking on the radio about a scientist.
Why does he visit places with extreme climates?
A He wants to find out how life on Earth began.
B He prefers being outdoors instead of in a laboratory.
C He wants to see how people live in extreme conditions.

3 You overhear a conversation between friends.
What are they talking about?
A a homework exercise
B a crossword
C a board game

4 You hear someone introducing an art course.
What does he want the students to learn?
A how to paint as they did when they were children
B how to paint with pleasure and confidence
C how to experiment with different colours

5 You hear a young man talking about writing his first song.
How did he feel while he was writing it?
A in love
B embarrassed
C angry

6 You hear an interview with a woman.
What's her job?
A a cheese maker
B a meat supplier
C a dairy farmer

7 You hear a conversation about buying a present.
What do they decide to buy?
A boots
B a DVD
C a book

8 You hear someone talking about music.
When does he think it is best to start learning a musical instrument?
A at as early an age as possible
B before you are ten
C when you are an adult

Speaking

Part 2

1 ▶11 Look at the photos and the question above them. Then listen to what the examiner says. Are the sentences true or false?

1 Each candidate talks about a single photo.
2 Each candidate asks a question about the other candidate's photos.
3 Each candidate has to compare two photos.

> Why do you think the people have chosen to go to these different places?

2 Identify these things in the photos.

exhibit	hall	gallery	installation
painting	sculpture	skeleton	showcase

3 ▶12 Listen to Candidate A talking about one of the photos. Answer the questions.

1 Which photo is she talking about?
2 Which of the expressions in the box below does she use?

●●● Speculating

I (don't) imagine that …
It's likely that …
I doubt that …
I (don't) suppose that …
I'd say / I wouldn't say that …
I should / shouldn't think that …

4 In pairs, complete Candidate A's answer. Talk about the other photo, contrasting it with the first. Use the phrases in 3 to help you.

5 In pairs, answer the examiner's question for Candidate B: *Which of these museums would you prefer to go to? Why?*

Use of English

Part 2 Open cloze

1 Read the rules about articles in the Grammar Reference (page 163) then match each underlined word or phrase in a–j below with one of the rules.

a He swam across <u>the English Channel</u> and climbed <u>Ben Nevis</u>, the highest mountain in <u>Britain</u>, in the same week. That's <u>an amazing achievement</u>.

b <u>After Easter</u> I'll be spending most of my time <u>at home</u>.

c I've got <u>a cat</u> and <u>a dog</u>. <u>The cat</u> is called Freddie and <u>the dog</u> is called Buster.

d Thomas Edison was <u>a</u> great scientist and inventor.

e <u>The British</u> have a reputation for being reserved.

f The longest river in <u>the world</u> is <u>the Amazon</u>.

g I always listen to <u>the radio</u> in <u>the morning</u>.

h I can't stand <u>modern art</u>.

i <u>After dinner</u> Kate played some tunes on <u>the piano</u>.

j John lives in <u>Nice</u>, <u>a city</u> on <u>the south coast</u> of <u>France</u>.

2 Quickly read the text below and find

a the name of the artist

b the name of someone with whom he worked

c two things he designed.

3 Read the text again carefully. Then read the **tip** box and complete gaps 1–8 with one word each.

4 Explain the use or non-use of articles in these phrases from the text.

a a man (l. 1)

b at school (l. 7)

c the Duke (l. 13)

d to France (l. 14)

e the greatest (l. 16)

f the world (l. 17)

tip In this text, gaps 1, 2 and 5 need an article.

RENAISSANCE MAN

LEONARDO DA VINCI was a man before his time, and (0) _was_ considered to be a genius. He became renowned for his multiple talents: he was (1) _____ painter, architect, engineer,
5 mathematician and inventor.

He was born in Vinci, near (2) _____ Italian city of Florence, in 1452. While he was at school, his teachers quickly noticed his curiosity and his inquiring mind. (3) _____ a youngster, he also displayed a
10 talent for drawing. On reaching his fourteenth birthday, Leonardo was apprenticed to Verrochio, a master painter and sculptor, (4) _____ studio was in Florence. Then he worked for the Duke of Milan and later moved to France, where he died in 1519, at
15 (5) _____ age of 67.

He is widely regarded as (6) _____ of the greatest painters in the world. As an engineer and inventor, he was ahead (7) _____ his time. He drew designs for machines that would only be invented centuries later,
20 (8) _____ as a helicopter, a calculator, and a tank.

Vocabulary

Phrasal verbs with *take*

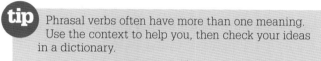

1 Read the dictionary entry for *take back* and match each sentence with one of the meanings.

> ,take sb↔'back to allow sb, such as your husband, wife or partner, to come home after they have left because of a problem ,take sb 'back (to...) to make sb remember sth: *The smell of the sea took him back to his childhood.* ,take sth↔'back **1** ⟳ if you **take** sth **back** to a shop/store, or a shop/store **takes** sth **back**, you return sth that you have bought there, for example because it is the wrong size or does not work **2** to admit that sth you said was wrong or that you should not have said it: *OK, I take it all back!*

Oxford Advanced Learner's Dictionary, 8th edition

a   This dress is too big. I'll have to take it back.

b   I don't know why she's agreed to take him back after he walked out on her like that.

c   He accused me of lying, but he later took it back and apologized.

d   That song takes me back to my time at college.

tip Phrasal verbs often have more than one meaning. Use the context to help you, then check your ideas in a dictionary.

2 Complete each pair of sentences with one of these words to form phrasal verbs.

> apart   in   off   on   up

a   I tried to listen as he gave me the bad news, but I couldn't take _____ what he was saying.
He lost a lot of money when he was taken _____ by an email claiming to be from a charity.

b   We collapsed in laughter when Fred took _____ the headmaster.
Mobile phones really took _____ in the 1990s.

c   The company has relocated to New York and taken _____ 20 new staff.
Jeff has taken _____ far too much work this year and has almost no free time.

d   We'll have to take the wardrobe _____ before we try to move it downstairs.
Italy took France _____ in the football final, beating them 4–0.

e   Ian plays the piano beautifully, but he didn't take it _____ until he was in his forties.
The sleeves on this jacket are too long. Can you take them _____ for me?

3 Match these verbs and phrases with the meanings of the phrasal verbs in 2.

a   agree to do
b   become successful
c   deceive
d   take to pieces
e   easily beat

f   employ
g   understand
h   pretend to be someone
i   shorten
j   start

Writing

Part 2 A review

1 Discuss these questions in pairs.

   a Who's your favourite actress and actor?

   b What do you like about them?

   c Which, in your opinion, is the best film they've appeared in? Why?

2 Look at the words and phrases in the box below and discuss these questions.

   a Do you like action films? Why/Why not? Do you have a favourite one?

   b Which of these words and phrases are typical of action films? Give examples from particular films.

> special effects   car chases   convincing stories
> exotic locations   villains   stunts   romance
> gripping   light-hearted   funny   violent

3 Read the film review opposite and say in which paragraph the writer mentions a–d.

   a aspects of the film they liked and disliked

   b their overall opinion and recommendation to the reader

   c background detail, i.e. the title, type of film, etc.

   d a brief description of the plot

4 What tense is used to describe the story?

5 Complete the gaps in sentences a–h with these words.

> fan   impressed   miss   performances   set
> short   spectacular   stands   tells   worth

   a There are some excellent _____ from the leading actors in the latest *Bond* film.

   b *Oblivion* is _____ in New York.

   c What particularly _____ me about *The Great Gatsby* was the acting.

   d If you're a _____ of sci-fi films, you won't be disappointed. *Star Trek Into Darkness* is well _____ seeing.

   e I've seen a lot of good films, but there's one that _____ out from the rest.

   f In _____ , *Waste Land* is quite simply the best documentary film I've ever seen. You really shouldn't _____ it.

   g *United 93* _____ the story of what might have happened on the United Airlines Flight on 11th September 2001.

   h The animated film *Despicable Me 2* is _____ to watch because of the amazing special effects.

FILMREVIEW

Iron Man 3

I'm not a great fan of action films so I wasn't expecting to enjoy *Iron Man 3*. However, I was pleasantly surprised by this action-packed follow-up to the first two *Iron Man* films.

The plot isn't particularly sophisticated. It revolves around an attempt by the shadowy villain Mandarin (Ben Kingsley) to launch terror attacks on the United States, and Iron Man's (Robert Downey Junior) superhuman efforts to foil his plans.

The acting is first-rate, as you would expect from stars like Downey Jr, Kingsley and Gwyneth Paltrow, and they are well supported by the rest of the cast. The script is witty and clever, with lots of snappy dialogue and many amusing moments. Visually the film is superb, with spectacular special effects that are a hallmark of the *Iron Man* movies.

Overall, *Iron Man 3* is highly entertaining. It isn't a deep or complex film, but as a two-hour action movie, I can't fault it. I can wholeheartedly recommend it to almost anybody.

6 Say which sentences in 5 could be used in a film review to

a introduce the film.

b describe the story.

c describe the acting.

d describe what it looks like.

e recommend the film.

how to do it

Divide your review into four paragraphs:

1 introduction (basic information, e.g. title, type of film, actors, director)

2 brief outline of the plot using the present simple – but don't give away the ending!

3 why you liked the film (acting? story? music? special effects? etc.)

4 your overall opinion and recommendation to see it.

7 Read the exam task below and the **how to do it** box. Then write a review (140–190 words) in an appropriate style. Include language from this section.

> You recently saw this notice in a film magazine called *Silver Screen*. Write a review.

FILMREVIEWS

Have you seen a good film recently? Write a review telling us why you liked it and send it to *Silver Screen Magazine*.

We'll publish the best reviews in next month's issue.

Review

1 Read the definitions and complete the adjectives that can be used to describe films.

a l _ _ _ _ - h _ _ _ _ _ _ (not very serious)

b s _ _ _ _ (frightening)

c p _ _ _ _ _ _ _ (creating a strong impression)

d g _ _ _ _ _ _ _ (very exciting and interesting)

2 Complete sentences a–g with phrasal verbs 1–7 in the correct form.

a They had to .... the computer system when a virus infected it.

b Who are those boys that are .... on the corner of the street?

c The interview .... well but then they asked me some questions that I couldn't answer.

d Can you .... your bag? Someone will trip over it if you leave it there.

e I need to .... a good title for my essay. Any suggestions?

f We couldn't get a table at the restaurant so we .... getting a take-away.

g 'If you don't do as I say,' said the wicked witch, 'I'll .... you .... a frog.'

1	end up
2	hang around
3	pick up
4	shut down
5	start off
6	think up
7	turn into

3 Complete the text using *a/an*, *the* or no article.

LENNON and McCARTNEY

John Lennon and Paul McCartney are considered by some to be (1)_____ greatest songwriting team of (2)_____ past 50 years. They were brought up in (3)_____ Liverpool in England in (4)_____ 1940s and 50s. While he was still at (5)_____ school, Lennon formed (6)_____ group called *The Quarrymen*. One day in 1956, (7)_____ group were playing at (8)_____ church fête when (9)_____ talented young musician called Paul McCartney was introduced to John. They began writing (10)_____ songs together in 1957. They would sometimes miss (11)_____ school and go to Paul's house while his father was at (12)_____ work. There they would make up (13)_____ tunes on (14)_____ piano. It was (15)_____ beginning of (16)_____ wonderfully creative partnership. In (17)_____ following thirteen years they wrote over 100 songs together before *The Beatles* finally split up in 1970.

4 Complete the missing part of the phrasal verbs in sentences a–k. Use each word below twice.

apart   back   in   off   on   up

Example   These jeans are a bit too long so I'll have to take them *up* .

a Don't be taken .... by his promises. He never keeps his word.

b The bed is too big to get through the door. Can you give me a hand to take it ....?

c He's great at impersonating people. He can take .... anybody.

d Our new DVD player didn't work so I took it .... to the shop.

e We can't take .... any more people because we haven't got any free office space.

f The smell of the sea always takes me .... to my childhood.

g Don't take .... any more work. You've already got more than you can cope with.

h In the 1950s, rock 'n' roll really took .... in the USA.

i If you're in London, give me a ring and we can take .... a film or a show.

j If you're bored with life, why don't you take .... a new hobby?

k Brazil have a much stronger team than England, so they will probably take them ....

Real or fake?

5

Lead in

1 Read the questionnaire below, then complete the gaps with these words.

cheated   forgery   honest   lie   own up
pretend   tell   truth   truthfully

HOW HONEST ARE YOU?

1 You're having dinner at a friend's house. The friend serves a dish that you really don't like, and says 'I hope you like it'. Would you _____ to like it?

2 A friend has a new haircut. You think it looks terrible. Your friend asks: 'What do you think of my new hair cut?' Would you answer _____?

3 A friend has fallen in love with somebody you don't like. Your friend asks you what you think of this person. Would you be _____ with your friend?

4 You accidentally crack a valuable ornament at somebody's house. Nobody sees you do it. Would you _____?

5 You know that a classmate _____ in an exam. Your teacher suspects that this is the case, and asks you if you know anything. What would you say?

6 A relative gives you a shirt as a present. You don't like it, so you give it away. The relative then asks you how often you wear the shirt. Would you _____ a lie?

7 You buy a ticket for a big football match from a stranger. Later you notice that it's a _____. Do you still try to get into the match?

8 You're at a boring party and you decide to leave. The host, who isn't a close friend, asks you why you are leaving. Would you tell the _____?

9 You and your parents are planning a surprise birthday party for your grandfather this Saturday. Your grandfather asks if you have any plans for the weekend. Would you _____ to your grandfather?

2 In pairs, answer the questionnaire together, then discuss your answers, giving reasons.

3 Think about your answers to the questionnaire. Try to summarize your opinions by completing the sentence below, then compare answers.

It is OK to tell a lie if …

Reading

Part 7 Multiple matching

1 In pairs, discuss the meanings of a–h and match words with similar meanings.

  a   a con
  b   a fraud
  c   genuine
  d   an impostor
  e   pose as
  f   legitimate
  g   pretend to be
  h   a trick

2 You are going to read a text about five impostors. Before you do, think of as many reasons as you can why someone might become an impostor.

3 Read the text opposite to find out if any of the people became impostors for the reasons you thought of in 2.

4 Read the text again carefully and for questions 1–10, choose from the people (A–E). The people may be chosen more than once.

Which person

  1   had to act as though they were younger than their real age?
  2   came into contact with a member of a royal family?
  3   used their professional skills to make people's lives better?
  4   pretended to be a member of a ruling family?
  5   invented a story about their past which involved an accident?
  6   spent some time in prison?
  7   was not an easy person to get on with?
  8   pretended to be several different people throughout their life?
  9   helped businesses to stop people dishonestly taking money from them?
  10 was a very influential and popular public speaker?

5 Imagine that you could lead somebody else's life for one week. Whose life would you choose and why? What would you do in that week?

IMPOSTORS

A Doctor James Barry

Having graduated from Edinburgh University in 1812, James Barry became a surgeon in the British Army. Although he was difficult and argumentative, Barry worked hard to
5 improve conditions for the troops and for ordinary citizens wherever he was staying. For example, when he was stationed in South Africa, he developed ways of improving the town's supply of clean water. Barry returned
10 to Britain in 1864. After his death, a post mortem examination revealed that James Barry was in fact a woman. It isn't clear why Barry chose to live as a man, but at that time a woman could not have had a career as an
15 army doctor. Being an impostor allowed Barry to help thousands around the world.

B Frédéric Bourdin

When 15-year-old Francisco began studying at Jean Monnet College in France, he claimed that he had just arrived from Spain. He said
20 that he had been an orphan since 2000, when his parents had died in a car crash. But it was all a lie. Francisco was in fact a 31-year-old Frenchman called Frédéric Bourdin. The school only realized the truth
25 when one of the teachers saw Bourdin on TV, in a documentary about impostors. The school principal, Claire Chardourne, said that the pupil had appeared a bit older than his classmates but she also said that Bourdin
30 had played the part brilliantly. Bourdin has confessed that he loved the attention he could get by pretending to be a teenager.

C Frank Abagnale

In 1964, at the age of 16 Frank Abagnale ran away from home to New York City. He used various cons to get money from
35 banks, changing his identity when they discovered his tricks. For two years he pretended to be an airline pilot with Pan Am and used a forged ID card to travel around the world free on their planes. Later, he changed his name to Frank Conners, and posed as a doctor, even though he had no qualifications. Over a
40 period of five years, Abagnale used eight different identities and committed fraud in 26 different countries. He was finally arrested, but on his release from jail after several years, Abagnale began a new, legitimate and very successful career as an adviser to banks on how to combat fraud!

D Grey Owl

45 In 1935, Londoners flocked to see a North American Indian called Grey Owl give lectures about the natural world. In over 200 lectures he addressed 250,000 people about the beauty and significance of the wild. He was incredibly popular and even gave a private talk to the King of England at Buckingham
50 Palace. Grey Owl, however, was not a genuine North American Indian at all. His name was Archibald Belaney and he was from England. When he was 18, he had gone to live in Canada, where he professed to be the child of an Apache mother. It was only after his death that his true identity became public. But
55 although Grey Owl was a fraud, he did a lot to educate and inspire people about the natural world.

E Anastasia Romanov

In the early 1920s a woman in a mental asylum in Berlin claimed that she was Anastasia, daughter of the Russian ruler Tsar Nicholas. It was widely believed that the whole family,
60 including Anastasia, had been killed by communist revolutionaries in 1918, but the location of the bodies was a mystery. Although a private investigation in 1927 concluded that the young woman was in fact Polish, she continued to maintain her claim until she passed away in 1984. However,
65 the subsequent discovery of Anastasia's body, and DNA tests carried out on it, proved beyond doubt that she was lying.

Vocabulary

Verbs connected with speech

1 Check the meaning of these words in a dictionary and put them into two groups: *loud* and *quiet*.

bellow	grumble	mumble	murmur
mutter	scream	shriek	shout	whisper

2 Choose the correct verb for these definitions.

a *bellow/shriek*: to shout in a high voice

b *mutter/whisper*: to speak quietly and unclearly

c *mumble/grumble*: to complain in a quiet voice

d *scream/shout*: to make a loud high cry from fear, pain or excitement

e *murmur/whisper*: to speak using only your breath, not your voice

3 Match sentence halves a–f with 1–6, choosing the correct prepositions.

a He's always *boasting about/for* …

b He finally *confessed to/at* …

c She always *insists in/on* …

d She often *complains about/with* …

e He *objected of/to* …

f He *begged* her *for/with* …

1 the best for her children.

2 another chance to prove his love.

3 his son's fantastic exam results.

4 the way his actions had been reported in the newspaper.

5 breaking my computer.

6 the noise from her neighbour's house.

4 Complete these sentences in an appropriate way.

a ' .... ,' the teacher grumbled.

b ' .... ,' the actor boasted.

c ' .... ,' the police officer insisted.

d ' .... ,' the photographer begged.

e ' .... ,' the waiter objected.

f ' .... ,' the impostor confessed.

g ' .... ,' the swimmer shrieked.

Grammar

Reported speech GR p168

1 Read the examples of direct speech and reported speech then answer questions a–c below.

1 'I don't want the rest of my pizza,' he insisted.
He insisted <u>that he didn't want the rest of his pizza</u>.

2 'You're standing on my toe,' she told him.
She told him <u>he was standing on her toe</u>.

3 'I'll phone you tomorrow,' she promised him.
She promised <u>that she would phone him the next day</u>.

4 'I only bought these shoes yesterday,' she complained.
She complained <u>that she had only bought the shoes the day before</u>.

a How do the tenses of the verbs change in each pair of sentences?

b How do these types of words change?
- personal pronouns (I, you, etc.)
- time expressions (today, tomorrow, etc.)
- possessive adjectives (my, your, etc.)
- demonstratives (this, that, etc.)

c Which word sometimes comes at the beginning of the underlined reported speech clauses, but is sometimes omitted?

2 ▶13 Listen to six people, then report what they say using reported speech. Choose the more appropriate of the reporting verbs given.

Example   'I'm trying my hardest!'

insist   agree
She insisted that she was trying her hardest.

Speaker 1	promise	warn
Speaker 2	complain	boast
Speaker 3	agree	boast
Speaker 4	beg	explain
Speaker 5	confess	predict
Speaker 6	warn	predict

3 Read reported questions 1–3 then answer a–d below.

1 She asked me where her new shoes were.

2 He asked her what she had done the previous day.

3 She asked them whether they wanted to come back the next day.

a Do reported questions follow the same word order as direct questions?

b Do reported questions use interrogative verb forms?

c What word introduces a reported question when there is no question word? (two possibilities)

d What were the original questions that the people asked?

4 Rewrite the dialogue below as reported speech.

Example Helen asked Mike what he was doing in her bedroom. Mike replied that …

Helen What are you doing in my bedroom?

Mike I'm looking for my mobile phone. Did you borrow it?

Helen I've never borrowed your mobile phone.

Mike You used it yesterday!

Helen I didn't make any calls. I was just looking for a phone number.

Mike Where did you leave it?

Helen I can't remember. Have you looked on the kitchen table?

Mike I've looked everywhere!

5 For a–f rewrite the reported speech with infinitives as direct speech.

a The neighbours asked him not to tell anyone.
'.. anyone.'

b The police ordered him to put his hands on his head.
'.. head.'

c His girlfriend told him not to worry about anything.
'.. anything.'

d Jenny agreed to help him with his homework.
'.. homework.'

e The managing director advised her to apply for the job.
'.. job.'

f The kidnappers warned him not to contact the police.
'.. the police.'

6 In pairs, tell each other about a–d.

a the most difficult thing that you've ever been asked to do

b the most surprising thing that anybody has ever told you

c something that you were always warned not to do as a child

d a promise someone didn't keep

7 Complete the newspaper article with the infinitive or other appropriate form of the verb in brackets. Add pronouns and other words if necessary.

BOBBY MASON was a celebrity in the small village of Southbourne where he lived. His neighbours often asked him ¹............ (tell) stories about his years as a top professional footballer in the 1960s. Bobby entertained them for hours. He told them ²............ (play) against George Best, one of the most famous footballers in the world at that time.

The problem was, it wasn't true. Although Bobby Mason was indeed the name of a footballer from the 1960s, the Bobby Mason in Southbourne had never been a footballer – he'd been a carpenter. When somebody told the real Bobby Mason what ³............ (happen), he was so angry that he drove to Southbourne and ordered the impostor ⁴............ (explain). The impostor admitted that ⁵............ (impersonate) the footballer, but claimed that it ⁶............ (start) by accident. 'People kept asking me if ⁷............ (be) the same Bobby Mason as the footballer. At first, I told them ⁸............ (not be), but when people kept asking, I almost started to believe it was true.'

Listening

Part 4 Multiple choice

1 Read the description opposite of a TV programme called *Faking It*. Which of the identities below do you think a female singer in a choir might be asked to take?

> a fashion photographer   a racing driver
> a rock singer   a television director

2 ▶14 Listen to an account of choirgirl Laura-Jane Foley's experiences in *Faking It* and answer these questions.

  a   Did you guess correctly in 1?

  b   Did Laura-Jane 'fake it' successfully?

3 ▶14 Listen again and choose the best answer for 1–7.

  1   How did Laura-Jane and the programme-makers first make contact?

     A   The programme-makers emailed lots of choir singers, including Laura-Jane.

     B   Laura-Jane phoned the TV company.

     C   The programme-makers went to see her choir.

  2   Laura-Jane was amazed that

     A   the programme-makers were interested in a Cambridge student.

     B   so many people from the TV company went to see her.

     C   the programme-makers started filming so soon.

  3   Laura-Jane's new identity was going to be

     A   BJ, lead singer of the band *Remake*.

     B   JJ, lead singer of the band *Reload*.

     C   LJ, lead singer of the band *Rehab*.

  4   According to Laura-Jane, why were arguments with Harry inevitable?

     A   Harry leads a real rock singer's lifestyle.

     B   Harry and Laura-Jane both have strong opinions.

     C   They only had four weeks for all the training.

  5   Laura-Jane thought her first rock concert

     A   was not very safe.

     B   was frightening but fun.

     C   was fun, but not something she'd want to do again.

  6   In what sense was Laura-Jane's training a failure?

     A   She didn't really change her style or attitude.

     B   She didn't enjoy the whole experience of becoming a rock singer.

     C   She didn't make the judges believe that she was a real rock singer.

  7   One positive result of the experience is that it made Laura-Jane

     A   change her views on life.

     B   become a more confident person.

     C   change her opinion of rock singers.

4 Look at the challenges in 1 again and discuss in pairs which one you would most like to try. Say why, and how successful you think you would be.

Faking It is a TV show which challenges people to adopt a completely new identity. Can they learn the new skills, style and attitude so well that, at the end of four weeks, even experts do not realize that they're faking it? There is always a big contrast between each person's real life and the new identity that they are asked to adopt. For example, in one programme, a quiet, shy chess player had to become the manager of a football team. And in another, a singer in a punk rock band became the conductor of a classical orchestra. The interesting part of the show is not only whether they manage to fool the experts, but also what they learn about themselves as people.

Speaking

Part 1

1 Read questions a–f below and in pairs brainstorm some ideas and words you might use to answer them.

   a What's your ideal holiday destination and why?

   b Are you a fan of new technology? Why/Why not?

   c Do you enjoy eating out? Why/Why not?

   d What can you tell about somebody from the way they dress?

   e Tell me about something that went wrong for you recently.

   f What are your earliest memories?

2 ▶15 Listen to five people answering questions from 1 and answer a–c.

   a Which question was not answered?

   b Did you hear any of the words from your list?

   c What other words gave away which question the speaker was answering?

3 ▶15 Listen again. Match each speaker from 2 to two of the phrases below, one from each language box.

●●● **Allowing** yourself time to think

Speaker	
....	I need to think for a moment.
....	That's an interesting question.
....	Well, it's difficult to say, really.
....	Let me see.
....	It depends what you mean, exactly.

●●● **Introducing** your answer

Speaker	
....	I guess the honest answer would be …
....	I suppose the simplest answer to that question is …
....	If I think about it, I suppose …
....	On balance, I think …
....	The best example that comes to mind is …

> **tip** In the exam, because you will not know what questions you are going to be asked, you may need to give yourself time to think before answering.

4 Work in pairs as Student A and B and do the following.

   • Student A ask B three of the questions from 1 and pay attention to the answers.

   • Student B answer two of A's questions honestly, but invent the answer to the other. Try to include phrases from 3 in your answers.

   • Student A try to guess which of Student B's answers was invented.

   • Swap roles so that Student B asks three questions.

Use of English

Part 3 Word formation

●●● Negative prefixes

Common negative prefixes in English are *un–*, *in–*, *im–*, *il–*, *ir–* and *dis–*. They can be added to certain verbs, but more often to adjectives and adverbs.

wrap – unwrap
aware – unaware
practical – impractical
appear – disappear
honestly – dishonestly

1 Read the information about negative prefixes. Then add negative prefixes to a–g, checking in a dictionary if necessary.

a   active
b   allow
c   legal
d   injured
e   possible
f   sane
g   sympathetically

2 Choose the correct word from those you formed in 1 to complete these sentences.

a   'Stop crying and go home,' she said ....

b   He was lucky to escape from the accident ....

c   In many countries it's .... to drive a car without wearing a seatbelt.

d   Why did the referee .... that goal? It looked OK to me!

e   According to Einstein, it's .... to travel faster than the speed of light.

f   The volcano had been .... for hundreds of years before it erupted.

g   You'd have to be .... to swim in that water – it's full of sharks!

3 Read the text opposite, ignoring the gaps, to find out what the two characters in the pictures have in common.

4 Read the **how to do it** box. Then read the text again carefully and complete gaps 1–8 with words formed from those below.

0   distinguish
1   aware
2   act
3   practical
4   technology
5   complete
6   likely
7   appear
8   questionable

● how to do it

Read the text once, ignoring the gaps, to find out what it is about.

Look at the context of each missing word and work out what part of speech it must be.

Find a word related to the base word which is the correct part of speech.

Read your completed text to check that it makes sense.

5 Does it matter whether you are watching a real actor or a computer-generated actor, if you can't tell the difference? Why/Why not?

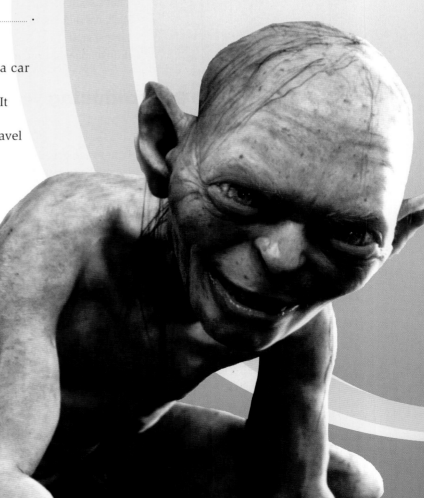

Vocabulary

Idioms connected with speech

1 Match expressions a–h with definitions 1–8.

a speak out against something
b speak your mind
c get to the point
d get the wrong end of the stick
e talk about someone behind their back
f talk down to someone
g talk someone into (doing) something
h talk someone out of (doing) something

1 say bad things about someone without them knowing
2 say publicly that something is bad
3 persuade someone not to do something
4 talk to someone as if they are not very intelligent
5 persuade someone to do something
6 misunderstand
7 say exactly what you think
8 begin the most important part of what you want to say

2 Complete sentences a–h with the correct form of the expressions in 1.

a She's a politician who .... all forms of injustice.
b Even though we were teenagers, some teachers still .... us, as if we were young children.
c My aunt insisted on taking three suitcases on holiday, even though we tried to .... it.
d My cousin took fifteen minutes to .... , and ask to borrow some money.
e I think you've .... – I only want to have dinner at this hotel, I don't need a room.
f Tanya was upset to find out that two of her best friends had been ....
g At first I didn't want to go skiing, but in the end my friends .... it.
h My dad is very direct. He always .... , even if it offends people from time to time.

C OMPUTER-GENERATED IMAGES are now so lifelike that they are almost **0** _indistinguishable_ from the real world. When audiences around the world watched the film *Titanic*, they were probably **1** .... that many of the actors were not human. The people falling from the ship as it sinks are in fact computer-generated **2** .... – or 'synthespians'. Using real people for these scenes would have been **3** .... and dangerous. More recent films have included computer-generated actors as main characters (for example, Gollum in *The Lord of the Rings*), or characters who are a mix of real and computer-generated images, such as Davy Jones in *Pirates of the Caribbean 2*. Eventually, **4** .... progress brought us *Avatar*, the first full-length film with a **5** .... computer-generated 3D world and 3D characters. However, it is **6** .... that computer-generated characters will ever cause all human actors to **7** .... But their **8** .... benefits surely mean that synthespians are here to stay.

Writing

Part 2 A report

1 In pairs, look at these words and answer the questions below.

congested	dilapidated	dreary	dull
extortionate	in (dire) need of renovation		overcrowded
overpriced	packed out	(extremely) run-down	
unaffordable	uninteresting		

    a Can you put the words and phrases into four groups with similar meanings?

    b Can you use some of the words and phrases to describe places in your own town or village?

2 Read the task and the report below, then explain the phrase 'warts and all' in your own words.

> A website called The Real Deal has asked you to write a 'warts and all' report of leisure facilities in your hometown. You should explain what leisure facilities are available and say what problems there are and how the facilities could be improved.

REPORT ON LEISURE FACILITIES IN EASTGATE

Introduction
The aim of this report is to given an honest description of the leisure facilities in Eastgate, including recommendations for their improvement.

Facilities

1 Sports
Facilities for sports in our town are very limited, in my opinion. There are some playing fields and a public swimming pool. The playing fields are fine if you want to jog, but there's not much else you can do there. The pool is very old and the changing rooms are in a terrible condition.

2 Eating out
The town has two well-known restaurants which serve lunch and dinner. The problem is, both restaurants are unaffordable for most ordinary teenagers. There is also a fast-food takeaway, but the food is greasy and there are no tables, so you can't eat in.

3 Entertainment
There's a fairly new cinema in Eastgate. Tickets are not too expensive, which is good, but the cinema only has two screens, so the choice of film is always limited. It's also very full at weekends.

Conclusion
The leisure facilities in Eastgate would be greatly improved by renovating the swimming pool and providing facilities for basketball and football at the playing fields. There is also a need for some more affordable places to eat and drink.

3 According to the report, what is wrong with the facilities in Eastgate? Use your own words, but include words and phrases from 1.

4 Complete sentences a–g with these words.

complaint	days	drawback	eyesore
lack	shame	trouble	

a The takeaway is popular with teenagers, so it's a .... that it doesn't open on Sundays or Mondays.

b There's a well-equipped gym at the secondary school, but it has one serious ....: it's only open to the general public at weekends.

c There's a dire .... of entertainment for people under 21.

d The shopping centre has seen better .... and many of the shops are empty.

e The main .... with the cinema is that the tickets are far too expensive.

f The department store was built in the 1970s and is a real ....

g The most commonly heard .... about the town centre is that there are too many buses and taxis.

5 Read the phrases in the language box below and find one which is used in the model answer.

●● Introducing recommendations

What (this town) could really do with is …
For me, the first priority would be …
I would very much like to see …
(This town) would be greatly improved by …
Nobody could deny that …
If it were up to me, I'd …

6 Use the phrases in the language box to make recommendations to address the problems in 4.

7 Read the **how to do it** box. Then answer the task in 2 by writing a report (140–190 words) about your own town. Include language from this section.

how to do it

Divide your review into sections:
1 an introduction which clearly states the purpose of the report
2 a main body (with subheadings if necessary) which contains the information required for the task
3 a conclusion which gives your overall opinion and / or recommendation (if the task requires)

Make sure your report directly addresses every point in the task. Write between 140 and 190 words.

Review

1 Complete sentences a–f with the most appropriate of these verbs.

> begged   boasted   confessed   insisted
> shouted   whispered

a   'I'm earning five times as much as my brother,' he _____ .

b   'I'm afraid I've lost those keys,' he _____ .

c   'I've seen this film before,' she _____ in his ear.

d   'My car is on fire!' she _____ .

e   'Please, please, stop singing!' he _____ .

f   'I really will be on time tomorrow,' he _____ .

2 Rewrite the sentences in 1 as reported speech.

3 Add negative prefixes to these words.

a   _____ civilized   e   _____ sincere
b   _____ accurate   f   _____ grateful
c   _____ logical   g   _____ tolerant
d   _____ probable   h   _____ loyal

4 Use the words from 3, with or without the negative prefix, to complete these sentences.

a   I'm very _____ for the help you have given me.

b   The earliest attempts to measure the size of the Earth were surprisingly _____ , given the lack of scientific instruments available at the time.

c   My parents are very _____ – they don't let me play loud music!

d   That dog was a _____ friend to me for 15 years.

e   It's _____ to choose to go on a cruise to the Arctic and then complain about the cold weather.

f   I believed everything you told me because I thought you were _____ .

g   It's rather _____ to wipe your nose on your sleeve.

h   Cars are a _____ cause of climate change.

5 Complete sentences a–e with an appropriate word.

a   I'm going bungee jumping and nobody is going to talk me _____ of it.

b   Martin Luther King Jr spoke _____ against racism.

c   I think I've got the wrong _____ of the stick. I thought you wanted to go out tonight?

d   Please get to the _____ – I haven't got all day!

e   Have you talked your parents _____ paying for your holiday?

6 Read the text and complete gaps 1–8 with words formed from those below.

0   discover
1   collect
2   examine
3   appear
4   believe
5   science
6   care
7   old
8   honest

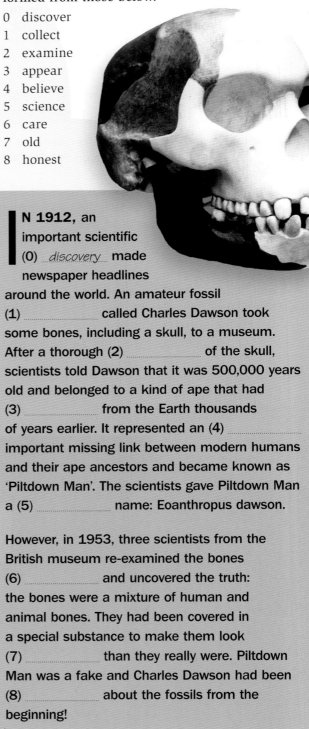

IN 1912, an important scientific (0) *discovery* made newspaper headlines around the world. An amateur fossil (1) _____ called Charles Dawson took some bones, including a skull, to a museum. After a thorough (2) _____ of the skull, scientists told Dawson that it was 500,000 years old and belonged to a kind of ape that had (3) _____ from the Earth thousands of years earlier. It represented an (4) _____ important missing link between modern humans and their ape ancestors and became known as 'Piltdown Man'. The scientists gave Piltdown Man a (5) _____ name: Eoanthropus dawson.

However, in 1953, three scientists from the British museum re-examined the bones (6) _____ and uncovered the truth: the bones were a mixture of human and animal bones. They had been covered in a special substance to make them look (7) _____ than they really were. Piltdown Man was a fake and Charles Dawson had been (8) _____ about the fossils from the beginning!

Journeys

Lead in

1 Look at the photos. Say whether or not you would enjoy these ways of travelling. Give reasons, thinking about the following and your own ideas.

- scenery
- comfort
- speed
- company

2 In pairs think of as many reasons as you can why people go on holiday. Discuss your ideas with another pair.

3 In many countries people are taking longer, more frequent and more expensive holidays than in previous generations. Why do you think this is? Think about

- work and pay
- the Internet
- cost of travel
- lifestyles and interests

Reading

Part 5 Multiple choice

Slovenian man's 5,265 km Amazon swim

Across the USA on a lawnmower

British women reach North and South Poles on foot

1 Read the newspaper headlines opposite. Discuss what problems these people might have faced on their journeys, and which you think was most difficult.

2 Read the text opposite quickly to find out what journey David Cornthwaite made. Think of a possible newspaper headline to describe it.

3 Match adjectives a–e with nouns 1–5, then check your answers in the text, and explain what the phrases mean.

a	epic	1	lorry
b	articulated	2	vehicle
c	constant	3	journey
d	four-wheel drive	4	speech
e	motivational	5	pain

4 Read the text again carefully and choose the best answers for 1–6.

1 Why did David Cornthwaite decide to skateboard across Australia?
   A He was an experienced skateboarder.
   B He wanted to break a world record.
   C He was bored with his life and wanted to try something different.
   D Somebody gave him a guidebook about Australia.

2 What made David fall off his skateboard several times in Australia?
   A thunderstorms in the Outback
   B the trains that race across the Outback
   C the injuries on his feet
   D the wind created by huge lorries going past

3 At times, David felt as though he
   A needed to stop for a while.
   B wanted to give up completely.
   C wanted to get out of the sun.
   D needed a new pair of shoes.

4 During the journey, where did David sleep at night?
   A in a four-wheel drive vehicle
   B in a tent
   C outdoors on the Nullarbor Plain
   D in the homes of his supporters

5 Why does David think surfing is a good thing to do after his journey?
   A He can stay close to Brisbane.
   B He's always wanted to surf on the Gold Coast.
   C He wants to strengthen the top half of his body.
   D He needs to keep his legs strong.

6 What does David hope to do eventually?
   A encourage other people to feel more positive about themselves
   B put his skateboard away
   C return to work as a designer
   D persuade other people to make long-distance journeys

5 Work in pairs. Role-play an interview with one of the people from the headlines in 1. Include these questions and add your own ideas.
   a 'How do you feel, now that you've finished your epic journey?'
   b 'What were the worst moments along the way?'
   c 'Have you got any similar treks in mind for the future?'

COAST TO COAST

A **27-year-old graphic designer** from Oxfordshire in England completed a record-breaking journey across Australia yesterday. It was a 5,800 kilometre odyssey – and he travelled the whole distance on a skateboard. David Cornthwaite, who started skateboarding less than two years ago, decided on his epic journey after waking up one morning and realizing he hated his job. 'I thought, the only thing keeping me going is the skate to and from work. I was a bit disillusioned and I was looking for something new,' he said. 'I saw a Lonely Planet guide to Australia. There was a map on the back. Perth was on one side and Brisbane on the other and I thought, "that'll do".'

He decided to prepare by skateboarding from John O'Groats to Lands End: the two points furthest apart on the British mainland. That 1,442-kilometre trek, which he finished in June, took just over a month, during which an infected blister swelled to the 'size of a tennis ball'.

Crossing Australia on a skateboard brought unique challenges. The wind caused by huge road trains, the articulated lorries that thunder across the Outback, was so powerful that he was sometimes blown off his board. Multiple blisters and aching ankles, toes and feet have kept him in almost constant pain for the last six weeks. 'I feel like an old man. I'm not sure that anyone has ever had this many blisters,' he said. Temperatures of 40°C and above mean that he has used more than a dozen tubes of factor 30 sunscreen. 'There have been moments where I thought "this is ridiculous, I have to rest", but I never contemplated giving up.' He has worn through 13 pair of shoes and has an over-developed right calf muscle which he compares to 'a giant chicken fillet'.

Skating an average of 50 kilometres a day and hitting speeds of up to 50kph on downhill runs, he left Perth, Western Australia, and skated across the fearsome Nullarbor Plain into South Australia. After reaching Adelaide he made his way to Melbourne and from there to Sydney. A support team of seven people trailed him all the way in a four-wheel drive vehicle, which included camping equipment for night stops. The journey has smashed the previous record for a long-distance skateboard, set by an American, Jack Smith, who covered 4,800 kilometres across the US in 2003.

David Cornthwaite was less than three kilometres from the end of his epic journey when he hit a hole and was thrown off his skateboard, suffering cuts and bruises to his shoulders, knees, hips and elbows. 'I was only going at 40kmh at the time, so although it wasn't pretty, it could have been a lot worse,' he said.

In the short term, he hopes to spend the next few days surfing on the Gold Coast, south of Brisbane, to build up some much-needed upper body strength. 'I've got huge legs but a skinny body – it's a bit ridiculous. I need to give my body a chance to warm down and surfing sounds ideal. For the time being I'm hanging up my skateboard.' In the longer term, he plans to give motivational speeches and write a book. Another long-distance journey is also on the cards. 'I'm certainly not going back to the day job,' he said.

Vocabulary

Travel

1 Decide which word does not belong in each of a–f. Say what connects the other three words.

 a platform   check-in   departure lounge   customs
 b hand luggage   baggage   overhead locker   suitcase
 c sail   wing   cabin   mast
 d bus driver   flight attendant   ticket inspector   propeller
 e barge   ferry   hovercraft   scooter
 f passport   ticket   ticket office   visa

2 Choose the correct verb in phrases a–f.

 a *to board/to mount* a plane
 b *to lift/to pick up* a passenger
 c *to get onto/to get into* a motorbike
 d *to change/to move* trains
 e *to cancel/to take away* a flight
 f *to get onto/to get into* a car

3 Complete the email with words and phrases from 1 and 2 in the correct form.

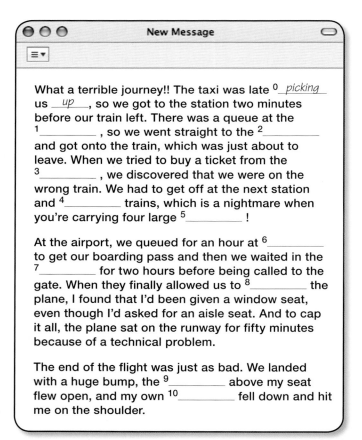

New Message

What a terrible journey!! The taxi was late [0] *picking* us *up*, so we got to the station two minutes before our train left. There was a queue at the [1]_____ , so we went straight to the [2]_____ and got onto the train, which was just about to leave. When we tried to buy a ticket from the [3]_____ , we discovered that we were on the wrong train. We had to get off at the next station and [4]_____ trains, which is a nightmare when you're carrying four large [5]_____ !

At the airport, we queued for an hour at [6]_____ to get our boarding pass and then we waited in the [7]_____ for two hours before being called to the gate. When they finally allowed us to [8]_____ the plane, I found that I'd been given a window seat, even though I'd asked for an aisle seat. And to cap it all, the plane sat on the runway for fifty minutes because of a technical problem.

The end of the flight was just as bad. We landed with a huge bump, the [9]_____ above my seat flew open, and my own [10]_____ fell down and hit me on the shoulder.

Grammar

Modal verbs: advice, ability, prohibition and obligation
GR p169–170

1 Choose the correct modal verb in sentences a–g.

 a You really *could/must* go to the Picasso Museum while you're in Barcelona – it's fantastic!
 b I don't think you *should/must* take the car. The shops are only a few hundred metres away!
 c You *can't/mustn't* lose your boarding pass. You *can't/mustn't* board the plane without it.
 d I think you *ought to/may* go by train – it's much faster than the coach.
 e Martin *should/could* see the train pulling away from the platform, but he *can't/couldn't* reach it in time.
 f You *can't/mustn't* drive when you're tired. It's dangerous.
 g To avoid risk of injury, passengers *must/may* remain seated during take-off and landing.

2 Read the sentences in 1 again and answer questions a–c.

 a Which three different modals can we use for giving advice, and which is the most emphatic?
 b Which modal do we use for obligation in its affirmative form, and prohibition in its negative form?
 c Which modal do we use to talk about ability in the past and what is its present tense form?

3 Work in pairs, Student A and Student B. Take it in turns to listen to your partner's problems and give advice, using a variety of appropriate modal verbs. Use the ideas below or your own.

A's problems
 • need to improve English – new job three months' time
 • argued with friend – won't answer phone calls
 • headaches every evening, especially using computer or TV

B's problems
 • interview next week – don't know anything about company
 • friend's birthday – haven't got any money
 • fancy dress party – Hollywood theme – can't think what to wear

4 Read the **tip** box. Then find and correct two examples in the text where *could* should be *managed to*.

I stood on the beach and waved my arms, shouting. Eventually, I could attract Harry's attention and he steered the boat in our direction. He couldn't come too close to the beach in case the boat became grounded, so we waded out to meet it. The waves were quite strong, and I could see that Jacqui was nervous. I remembered that Mark could swim, but Jacqui couldn't. I held her arm as the water became deeper. When the boat came alongside, I could grab hold of the ladder and hold it steady while she climbed aboard.

5 Complete sentences a–f with *must, mustn't, have/has to* or *don't have to*.

a You .... park there. It's for emergency vehicles only.

b You .... wear your seatbelt during the whole flight, but it's advisable to keep it fastened while you're in your seat.

c Please note that all passengers .... check in at least 45 minutes before the scheduled departure time.

d There's no bus into town, so I always .... walk or cycle.

e People over 65 .... pay to travel by bus – it's free.

f These days, you .... smoke on any flight.

6 Complete the text below using modal verbs in the correct form. More than one answer may be possible.

Greener Travel

You are no doubt aware of the negative impact which international travel has on the environment, but you may not realize how much you ¹ .... do to minimize it. And you ² .... give up travelling altogether – you ³ .... make a difference just by taking a few simple measures.

Your efforts ⁴ .... start even before leaving home. You ⁵ ...... leave TVs, hi-fis and other electrical equipment on standby because that wastes a surprising amount of electricity.

While on holiday, you ⁶ ...... use public transport when available, rather than hiring a car. If you're staying in a hotel, remember that you ⁷ ...... have clean towels every day, you ⁸ .... easily re-use them. And of course, you absolutely ⁹ .... avoid buying souvenirs that are made from endangered species.

Listening

Part 1 Multiple choice

1 Look at travel problems a–f and decide which forms of transport they could apply to.

a The crossing was cancelled owing to bad weather.

b We had a flat tyre.

c The driver got lost.

d We ran out of petrol.

e We missed our stop.

f We couldn't find our tickets.

2 ▶16 You will hear people talking in eight different situations. Listen, and for questions 1–8 choose the best answer (A, B or C).

1 You hear a conversation in a travel agent's.
What is the customer's attitude?
A demanding
B indecisive
C complaining

2 You hear part of a radio documentary about a man who travelled through America.
How many different ways did Mark travel?
A by bike, on foot and by boat
B by bike and on foot
C by bike

3 You hear a weather forecast.
How many types of transport are mentioned?
A three
B four
C five

4 You hear a woman talking about a decision she made.
What was the main reason for her decision?
A to be different from everyone else
B to avoid boredom in her life
C to raise awareness of issues she cares about

5 You hear an inventor talking.
How long has he been working on his latest invention?
A since he was a boy
B since before his grandad's death
C since his visit to China

6 You hear two people talking.
How does the receptionist deal with the customer?
A unhelpfully
B unkindly
C impatiently

7 You hear Sally talking to her friend.
What is Sally's main problem?
A She's damaged her brother's bike.
B Her bike is broken.
C She's hurt her leg.

8 You hear two people talking.
Where are they?
A at a bus station
B at a railway station
C at an airport

tip Remember that in the exam there are eight unrelated texts.

3 In pairs, take it in turns to find out about your partner's worst travel experience. Use these ideas to help you.
• where they were going from and to
• what time of year it was
• who they were travelling with
• what form of transport they used
• how long the journey should have taken and how long it actually took

Speaking

Parts 3 and 4

1 ▶ 17 Listen to five short dialogues about trips and excursions from Cairo. Match three of them to photos 1, 2 and 3. Which words gave you the answers?

2 ▶ 17 Listen again and match two of phrases a–j to each dialogue (1–5).

a … seems like the best option to me. ☐
b If you ask me, I really think we should … ☐
c Personally, I'm in favour of … ☐
d Believe me, … ☐
e I'm sure it will be worth it. ☐
f Let's go for it. ☐
g … don't you agree? ☐
h I'm really keen on the idea of … ☐
i But just think of the … ! ☐
j Oh, come on! ☐

3 In pairs, look at the diagram and do the tasks. Use phrases from 2.

> Imagine you are on holiday in Cairo. Here are some of the excursions you could go on. Talk to each other about what you would find enjoyable or not enjoyable about these different excursions.

> What would be enjoyable or not enjoyable about these excursions from Cairo?

- a 30-minute helicopter flight over the pyramids
- a day trip to Alexandria
- a visit by camel to the tombs of the first pharaohs in Saqqara
- an evening cruise on the Nile
- a two-day desert safari by jeep

> Decide which two excursions you are going to book.

4 Discuss these Part 4 questions.

a What kinds of excursion do you prefer? Are you more interested in history or landscapes? Excitement or relaxation?

b In your opinion, what are the advantages of going on an organized excursion, as opposed to visiting a place independently? Are there any disadvantages?

c What are the most interesting excursions you could go on in your own country or region? Describe them.

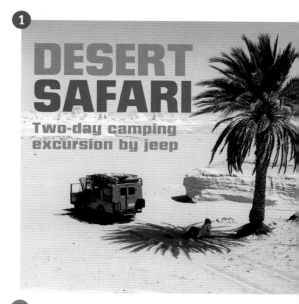

DESERT SAFARI
Two-day camping excursion by jeep

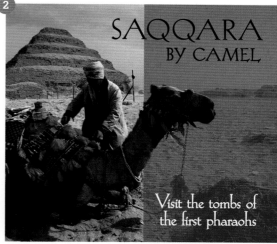

SAQQARA BY CAMEL
Visit the tombs of the first pharaohs

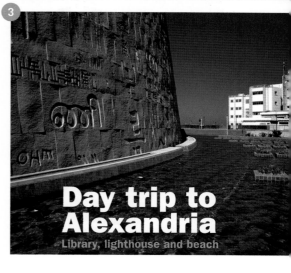

Day trip to Alexandria
Library, lighthouse and beach

Use of English

Part 4 Key word transformations

1 For each of a–f, decide which of 1–6 below can replace the words or phrases in bold.

a   Please leave your mobile number at reception **so that** we can contact you in an emergency.

b   I couldn't remember **if** I'd left my key in my hotel room.

c   This room does not look **as if** it has been cleaned.

d   The café is open all day, **while** the main restaurant only opens at meal times.

e   We may as well have breakfast, **seeing that** it's included in the room rate.

f   The hotel has a gymnasium **and** a swimming pool.

1   as though
2   as well as
3   in order that
4   since
5   whereas
6   whether

2 Read the example. Then, for each of a–f, write a sentence with the same meaning. Replace the word in bold with a word or phrase with the opposite meaning, and make any other changes necessary.

Example   Her parents won't buy her a car unless she **passes** her driving test.

passes → fails   (unless → if)

Her parents won't buy her a car if she fails her driving test.

a   Passengers must not **stand** while the coach is moving.

b   Phone me if you know that your flight won't be **on time**.

c   Travelling by bus is **cheaper** than travelling by taxi.

d   The more expensive seats are more **comfortable**.

e   When there's a lot of traffic, the journey is **slower**.

f   The use of mobile phones is **forbidden** during the flight.

3 Rewrite each sentence a–f keeping the meaning the same. Use two to five words, including the word given.

a   If the flight is on time, we should arrive at the hotel before 9 p.m.
   provided
   We should get to the hotel by 9 p.m. _____ late.

b   You might need to get a taxi, so take some money with you.
   case
   Take some money with you _____ to get a taxi.

c   This year's holiday was less enjoyable than last year's.
   fun
   Last year's holiday _____ this year's.

d   Travellers are not allowed to bring pets into the UK unless they have a 'pet visa'.
   only
   Travellers can _____ into the UK if they have a 'pet visa'.

e   The journey was better than I'd expected.
   bad
   The journey _____ as I'd expected.

f   That ferry seems to be leaning to one side.
   though
   That ferry looks _____ to one side.

Vocabulary

Idioms with *come* and *go*

1 Choose the correct verb to complete sentences a–h. Use a dictionary to check your answers and make sure you understand the meaning of the phrases in italics.

a I refused to pay the mechanic's bill in full because the work didn't *come/go up to scratch*.

b She'd always loved Tom Cruise, so meeting him at the film première was *a dream come/gone true*.

c *As far as* rooms *come/go*, it was OK, but it was nothing special.

d *When it comes/goes to* sailing, I know almost nothing.

e I can get by in French and Spanish, although languages don't *come/go easily to* me.

f My brother passed his driving test at the sixth attempt, which *just comes/goes to show* that you should never give up!

g We had a flat tyre just after we set off, and after that, the journey *came/went from bad to worse*.

h I tried to think of a clever reply, but nothing *came/went to mind*.

2 Read the text below, then rewrite the underlined parts (1–8) using phrases from 1.

As far as holidays are concerned (1) I usually choose something cheap, so you can imagine my surprise when my husband booked a cruise. Compared to most cruise ships (2) ours was not particularly large or luxurious, and we were disappointed that there were no staff to help us with our luggage. The situation got even worse (3), however, when we finally found our accommodation. It was small, badly furnished and dirty. What we thought of first (4) was a prison cell, not a luxury cabin. Like many people, I don't find it easy to complain (5), but on this occasion I had to say something because the accommodation simply wasn't satisfactory (6). Reluctantly, the staff agreed to move us to another, slightly more comfortable cabin, which proves (7) that complaining *can* work. But some of the passengers were heartbroken; they had been looking forward to the holiday of a lifetime, but this cruise was a nightmare rather than a really enjoyable experience (8).

Writing

Part 1 An essay

1 Read the task and model answer below. Answer these questions.

a What is the student's overall answer to the question in the essay title and where is it expressed?

b Does the essay cover points 1 and 2 from the notes in the task? Where?

c Which ideas in the essay are not mentioned in the notes?

In your English class you have been talking about the benefits and harm caused by global tourism. Now your English teacher has asked you to write an essay. Write an essay using *all* the notes and give reasons for your point of view.

Essay question

Is global tourism good for the world?

Notes

Things to write about
1 learning about the world
2 damage to the environment
3 your own idea

IS GLOBAL TOURISM GOOD FOR THE WORLD?

Global tourism has grown enormously in the past few decades, and each year millions of people travel to different countries for holidays. Is this new industry a good or bad thing for the world?

It is often said that travel broadens the mind, and it is certainly true that visiting other countries raises people's awareness of global issues like poverty and the environment. Furthermore, tourism provides an income for people who live in some of the poorest countries in the world.

That said, it cannot be denied that some forms of tourism are harmful to the environment. Firstly, there is the pollution caused by transport, especially aeroplanes. In addition, irresponsible tourism can sometimes spoil beautiful coastlines. But if governments are aware of this issue, they can make laws to prevent over-development. Individual tourists also need to consider what impact they are having on the environment.

In conclusion, I believe that the benefits of tourism for individuals and communities outweigh the disadvantages. However, tourists should be aware of the environment and choose eco-friendly holidays whenever possible.

2 Choose the correct verbs to complete these common expressions, then check your answers by finding them in the essay in 1.

a to *travel / visit* to other countries

b to *travel / visit* other countries

c to *rise / raise* awareness (of something)

d to *produce / provide* an income

e to *make / write* laws

f to *cause / have* an impact (on something)

3 In pairs, read the task below. Then discuss whether you agree or disagree with ideas a–f.

In your English class you have been talking about the advantages and disadvantages of taking holidays in your own country rather than abroad. Now your English teacher has asked you to write an essay. Write an essay using *all* the notes and give reasons for your point of view.

Essay question

Is it better to go on holiday in your own country or abroad?

Notes

Things to write about

1 impact on the environment

2 helping the economy

3 your own idea

a You can have a wide variety of experiences within your own country.

b It's more important to help the economy of countries poorer than your own country.

c It's impossible to travel abroad without damaging the environment.

d You should learn about different regions of your own country before you learn about other countries.

e Travelling abroad makes you a better language-learner.

f Staying in your own country is always cheaper than going abroad.

4 Decide on your overall answer to the question in the essay title. Plan your essay, following the same general pattern as the essay in 1:

paragraph 1   a few introductory ideas

paragraph 2   arguments which support your overall answer

paragraph 3   examples that support the opposite side of the argument

paragraph 4   your overall opinion to sum up

5 Decide in which paragraph or paragraphs of your essay you might be able to use each of phrases a–j.

a All things considered, …

b Having said that, …

c In addition, …

d In conclusion, I'd say that …

e Generally speaking, …

f On balance, I think …

g First and foremost, …

h On the other hand, …

i However, …

j To begin with, it's worth acknowledging that …

6 Read the phrases in the language box and find one which is used in the essay in 1.

●●● Introducing facts and opinions

| People often find that … |
| Some people believe that … but others insist … |
| It is true that … |
| It is often said that … |
| Nobody could deny that … |
| It is sometimes suggested that … |

tip When giving different points of view, avoid using I; instead use impersonal phrases like the ones in the language box.

7 Write an essay (140–190 words) in answer to the task in 3. Use ideas and language from 3, 4, 5 and 6. Add your own ideas if necessary.

Review

1 Complete the sentences with words from the box.

> bus driver   visa   ferry   flight attendant
> ticket   hand luggage   overhead lockers   scooter

a As well as a passport you'll also need a
_____ to enter many countries.

b Cars are not allowed on the _____ , but
you can take a bicycle or _____ .

c Please try to give the _____ the correct
money for your _____ .

d When we got on the plane, the _____ told
us to store our _____ in the _____ .

2 Choose the correct verb in sentences a–e.

a Our minibus seemed to stop every two minutes
to *board/pick up* more passengers.

b Is it a direct service, or do I need to *change/pick
up* trains in Boston?

c Ignoring the crowd of journalists, the minister
got into/got onto his car and drove off.

d It was impossible to leave New York by air that
night; the snow meant that all flights had been
cancelled/changed.

e Passengers must wait in the departure lounge
until it is time to *board/get into* the flight.

3 Rewrite sentences a–h to include an appropriate
modal verb. Do not change the meaning of the
sentences.

a It's essential for you to wear a helmet when
you're riding a motorbike.

b From our first floor apartment, we were able
to hear noises in the street below.

c It was impossible for us to reach the airport
in time.

d Is it OK for me to have a seat by the aisle?

e I advise you not to drink the tap water when
you're staying in a hotel.

f It isn't necessary for you to tell me, I already
know where you've been!

g Only seven students were able to finish the
exam within the time allowed.

h I recommend that she visits the Eye Museum
while she's in Brazil.

4 Complete gaps 1–6 in the text with these words
and phrases.

> as though   as well as   since
> in order that   whereas   whether

We were particularly keen to see leopards on our
safari. Elephants are quite common in this part
of Tanzania, (1) _____ zebra and antelope,
(2) _____ leopards are comparatively rare. (3) _____
leopards are nocturnal, it was recommended that we
go out in the jeep at night. We set off at dusk, and after
two hours without any luck, it really felt (4) _____ the
excursion was going to be a waste of time. Then
suddenly, we heard some movement in the bushes.
The driver turned off the engine (5) _____ the noise
wouldn't frighten the animals away, and we waited to
find out (6) _____ our dreams of seeing a leopard were
finally going to come true. And then, with a low growl, a
leopardess and her two cubs stepped into the clearing.

5 Complete the second sentence so that it has a
similar meaning to the first sentence, using the
word given. You must use between two and five
words, including the word given.

a The hotel room really wasn't satisfactory.
come
The hotel room really _____ scratch.

b It was a bumpy flight, and things got even
worse after we'd landed.
bad
It was a bumpy flight, and things _____ to
worse after we'd landed.

c When my parents asked what I wanted for my
birthday, I couldn't think of anything.
came
When my parents asked what I wanted for my
birthday, _____ mind.

d My sister is not bad at tennis, although she
doesn't find ball games easy.
easily
My sister is not bad at tennis, although ball
games _____ to her.

I get the message

Lead in

1 In pairs, discuss which of these forms of communication you can see in the photos. Then discuss which forms you use, when you use them, and who you communicate with.

a email
b letter
c postcard
d text message
e phone
f micro-blogging
g social networking
h instant messaging

2 Discuss these questions.

a Are each of a–h in 1 generally more popular with older or younger people? Why?

b What are the advantages and disadvantages of a–h in 1? Think about
   • cost
   • speed
   • convenience
   • degree of formality
   • the situation (e.g. personal or business)

c Which of a–h in 1 will become more popular in the future, and which less popular, in your opinion? Why?

Reading

1 Imagine you are lost in a remote place and need to signal for help to passing aircraft. Explain how these items might be useful.

2 Read the text opposite about emergency signals to check your ideas from 1. Explain the 'obvious reason' mentioned in the final sentence.

RESCUE!

We are used to having many forms of communication at our fingertips: mobile phones, email, instant messaging ... But imagine a situation in which you are alone in the wilderness, hoping to be rescued, with no way of calling for help. Here are some tips on
5 how to communicate with your potential rescuers.

A SOS

SOS is the best-known international distress signal. It is popularly believed to stand for 'Save Our Souls', but in fact the letters were chosen because they are easily transmitted and understood in Morse Code: three dashes followed by three dots, followed by three dashes
10 (– – – . . – – –). The signal can also be transmitted both visually and audibly. If you don't have a torch, you could use rocks or branches to spell out the code on the ground.

B SMOKE SIGNALS

During the hours of darkness, fires are the most effective method of signalling. Three fires in a triangle are an international distress signal
15 which pilots and rescue workers everywhere will understand. If you are in a jungle or forest, find a clearing, otherwise the fires will not be visible from very great distances. A burning tree is another way of attracting attention. During the day, fires are also a good way of signalling, provided that they are producing a lot of smoke. Think
20 about what colour the smoke should be in order to stand out against the background. Adding green vegetation to the fire produces white smoke; adding rubber (for example, an old tyre) or oil produces black smoke.

C MIRROR SIGNALS

On a sunny day, the most effective method of signalling is a mirror. In
25 fact, pilots have reported seeing mirror flashes up to 160 kilometres
away. If you do not have a mirror, any shiny metal surface may work.
Aim the mirror by holding up one finger of your other hand in line with
the aircraft. If you can hear an aircraft but can't see it because of
cloud, shine the mirror in the direction of the noise. Be careful not to
30 shine the mirror at the aircraft's cockpit for more than a few seconds,
as it might temporarily blind the pilot. And if you are in a war zone,
do not flash the mirror rapidly or the pilot may mistake the signal for
gunfire and avoid the area – or worse, return fire!

D LONG RANGE GROUND-TO-AIR SIGNALS

Once you have been seen by an aircraft, it may be necessary to
35 exchange vital information. The person on the ground can create
symbols by any means possible – leaves, branches, marks on the
snow. They must be visible from the air. This usually means at least
three metres long and a metre wide. A single line means 'serious injury,
doctor required', while two capital Ls mean 'all is well'. If you have a
40 large area of cloth, such as a sail or life-raft cover, you can fold it into
various patterns to give information. Folding one corner means 'we
need fuel, but our plane is flyable'. Folding two corners means 'we
need warm clothing'.

E BODY SIGNALS AND PILOT'S REPLIES

When the aircraft is close enough for the pilot to see you clearly,
45 use body movements to convey a message. Raising both hands above
your head means 'pick us up' if you keep them still, or 'do not attempt
to land here' if you move your hands to the side in an arc. If the pilot
has seen and understood your signal, he or she will make the aircraft
rock from side to side so the wings go up and down. If, however, the
50 message has been seen but not understood, the aircraft will fly in
a clockwise circle overhead. For obvious reasons, there is no signal
which means 'message not seen'!

3 Read the text again carefully.
For questions 1–10, choose from
the sections A–E. The sections
may be chosen more than once.

Which section mentions a
signal which

1   should be in a different
    colour according to the
    situation?
2   can potentially be seen from
    very great distances?
3   can only be used when an
    aircraft is very near?
4   is the best one to use after
    sunset?
5   is sometimes mistakenly
    thought to represent a series
    of words?
6   could be mistaken for an
    attack by the person sending
    it?
7   could be made with a large
    piece of material?
8   may be effective even if the
    sky is not clear?
9   does not require any special
    equipment or materials?
10 can be used to request
    delivery of specific items?

4 In pairs, discuss the best way
of making emergency signals
in these different places.
  • a rainforest
  • a desert
  • a mountain range
  • a grassy plain

Vocabulary

The verb *get*

tip *get* is a very common verb, especially in spoken English. It has a number of meanings and is used with prepositions and particles to form many phrasal verbs.

1 In three minutes think of as many meanings as you can for the verb *get*. Compare your answers in pairs, then check in a dictionary.

2 Match 1–7 below with the meanings of *get* in sentences a–g.

  a I don't get that joke.

  b In Iceland it doesn't get dark until about 11 or 12 o'clock in the summer.

  c I got a 'B' in my maths exam.

  d She always gets hay fever in the summer.

  e I can never get my younger daughter to eat any fruit.

  f What time did you get here?

  g We're getting a new washing machine next week.

1	suffer from (an illness)
2	understand
3	make (someone do something)
4	achieved
5	become
6	arrive
7	buy

Grammar

Passives GR p170–171

1 Read the newspaper article about mobile phone crime, then complete the text beneath it with active verbs instead of passives.

Theft of mobiles on the increase

A NATIONWIDE CRACKDOWN on mobile phone crime in Britain is being carried out by police. A police spokesperson said it was believed that 50% of all street crime involved the theft of a mobile phone. Over 200 mobile phones an hour are thought to have been stolen in Britain last year. Many of them are exported by gangs to Europe, Asia and Africa. Stolen phones can be blocked by the phone networks for use in Britain, but SIM cards can sometimes be replaced by thieves to make phones usable abroad. An international database has been set up by the phone companies to try to make all stolen handsets useless, whatever their destination. In future, the details of all stolen handsets will be shown on this database so that the phones can be blocked internationally as well as within Britain.

Police (1) .... a nationwide crackdown on mobile phone crime in Britain. A police spokesperson said they (2) .... that 50% of all street crime involved the theft of a mobile phone. Police (3) .... that over 200 mobile phones an hour were stolen in Britain last year. Gangs (4) .... many of them to Europe, Asia and Africa. The phone networks (5) .... stolen phones for use in Britain, but the thieves can sometimes (6) .... SIM cards to make phones usable abroad. The phone companies (7) .... an international database to try to make all stolen handsets useless, whatever their destination. In future, this database (8) .... the details of all stolen handsets so that the phones can be blocked internationally as well as within Britain.

2 Complete these extracts from radio reports using the correct verbs in the passive form.

> hold   catch   arrest   discover

'A man **1**_____ by police last night after he **2**_____ shoplifting in a local store. Several thousand pounds' worth of jewellery **3**_____ in his pockets. He **4**_____ in police custody until he appears in court tomorrow.'

> convict   fine   find   stop

'Carl Hancock, a retired doctor, **5**_____ £3,000 after **6**_____ of drunken driving. His car **7**_____ by police officers on the motorway and he **8**_____ to have 150 milligrammes of alcohol in his blood, almost twice the legal limit.'

3 Find examples of *subject + modal verb + passive infinitive* in the article in 1. Then complete a–f using the passive infinitive and the words in brackets.

a This film _____ (can/see) at cinemas all over the country.

b In Japan, shoes _____ (must not/wear) in the house.

c The new football stadium _____ (should/complete) before 2012.

d The 9/11 terrorists _____ (should never/be allowed) onto the planes.

e John F Kennedy _____ (might not/kill) by Lee Harvey Oswald.

f Look at the postmark. This letter _____ (must/post) in London.

4 Find examples of these structures in the article in 1.

a *It* + passive + *that* clause

b subject + passive + infinitive

5 Rewrite sentences a–f in the passive, as in the example.

Example   In the past people thought that swimming in the sea was bad for you.

In the past it was thought that swimming in the sea was bad for you.

In the past swimming in the sea was thought to be bad for you.

a Someone reported that a coach collided with a lorry on the motorway last night.

b They thought the politician was telling the truth.

c People believe the police have arrested the wrong man.

d They expect that Mary will pass all her exams.

e People consider that he is one of the finest writers alive.

f They believe that the woman was driving too fast when she crashed into the tree.

6 Read sentences 1 and 2 below and answer these questions.

a How many objects does *owe* have in sentence 1? Which is the direct object and which is the indirect object?

b In sentence 2, which object becomes the subject of the passive verb: the direct object, or the indirect object?

1 My brother owes me £50.

2 I'm owed £50 by my brother.

7 Make sentences a–e passive as in the example. Include the agent, thinking carefully about its best position in the sentence.

Example   My boss offered me a promotion at work.

I was offered a promotion at work by my boss.

a Mr Fielding teaches us English.

b The online store will send me a receipt in the post.

c The kidnappers have given him two days to pay the ransom.

d My wife read the children a bedtime story.

e Her secretary brought her two letters to sign.

Listening

Part 3 Multiple matching

1 ▶18 You will hear five people talking about misunderstandings. Match the speakers with misunderstandings A–H. There are three extra letters.

Speaker 1 ....
Speaker 2 ....
Speaker 3 ....
Speaker 4 ....
Speaker 5 ....

A went to the wrong meeting place
B invited the wrong person to a meeting
C misheard directions to a place
D misunderstood some instructions
E misunderstood an invitation
F went to a meeting they weren't invited to
G gave a talk on the wrong topic
H gave someone the wrong information

2 ▶18 Complete sentences a–f from the recording with the correct phrasal verb, then listen again and check your answers.

a So we .... off and I didn't bother to check where we were going on the map.
b We got hopelessly lost because I'd .... down the wrong road.
c What <u>was</u> a problem was that Becky didn't .... up.
d It .... out that they needed to discuss what projects they were going to give me!
e He said they usually .... together with some old friends from university, but why didn't we .... round for a drink.
f There was a big sales conference .... up.

3 In pairs, tell each other about a misunderstanding that you have been involved in. Use the phrases below to help you.

- I was under the impression that ...
- I thought that ... but in fact ...
- Naturally I assumed that ...
- It turned out that ...
- It was so embarrassing.
- I was horrified.
- I felt awful.
- I felt such a fool.
- We had a good laugh about it.

Speaking

Parts 3 and 4

1 What would be the advantages of doing a language course in an English-speaking country, rather than in your own country? Would there be any disadvantages?

2 In pairs, look at the poster below and decide whether these images would be successful in attracting teenagers to the language school. Give reasons.

3 ▶19 **Listen to a dialogue about the poster. Do you agree with their choice of slogan?**

4 ▶19 **Listen again. Match the two halves of these sentences from the dialogue.**

1 If you ask me,
2 To be honest,
3 The way I look at it,
4 The thing is,
5 Let's face it,
6 Don't forget,

a parents will want to know the teachers are qualified.
b not all teenagers enjoy going to discos anyway.
c parents need to feel their children are being looked after well.
d the parents will be paying for everything.
e teenagers aren't that interested in the countryside.
f most teenagers like the idea of making friends.

5 **Look at the diagram. Then do the tasks below.**

Imagine you are designing a poster for a language school. Discuss how successful each feature would be in attracting 14- to 16-year-olds to a summer course.

How successful would these slogans be in attracting 14- to 16-year-olds to a summer course?

Fantastic sports and leisure facilities

Classes delivered using latest technology

Twice-weekly excursions included in price

Central location close to shops and museums

Host families with teenage children

Decide which two features should be mentioned on the poster.

6 ▶20 **Listen to two students doing a Part 4 task. Tick the questions the examiner asks and say which candidate gives better answers.**

a Would you like to take a course at this language school?
b What are the advantages and disadvantages of studying English abroad?
c What are the advantages and disadvantages of having an English teacher who cannot speak your own language?
d Why do you think it's important to study foreign languages?

7 **Read the how to do it box. Then work in groups of three and follow these instructions.**

STUDENT A: You are the examiner. Ask some of the questions in 6. Involve both Students B and C in the discussion. Keep the discussion going for about three minutes.

STUDENTS B and C: You are the candidates. Answer the questions. Give reasons for your opinions.

how to do it

Listen to the examiner's questions.
Ask for repetition if necessary.
Give a full, confident answer.

Use of English

Part 1 Multiple-choice cloze

1 Rewrite sentences a–g replacing the underlined words with the correct form of these phrasal verbs. Use your dictionary if necessary.

> get at   get down   get in   get on   get out of
> get through   get up to

  a How did you <u>avoid</u> going to that dreadful party?

  b What page have you <u>reached</u> in the book you're reading?

  c We've <u>used</u> six litres of milk since your parents arrived.

  d Give me a break, will you? You're always <u>criticizing</u> me.

  e What really <u>depresses</u> me about winter is the long cold evenings.

  f What time does your flight <u>arrive</u>?

  g 'Grandad's getting very forgetful.' 'Well, he's <u>growing older</u>, isn't he?'

2 Quickly read the text opposite, ignoring the gaps. Has anything similar to the incidents described ever happened to you or someone you know?

EMAILS THEY WISH THEY'D NEVER SENT

EMAIL is an easy and fast (0) .... of communication – but sometimes just one little click of the 'send' button can spell disaster.

Emails can accidentally be sent to the (1) .... person, or to several people (2) .... just one person. Dave Gethings got (3) .... trouble when he sent a joking, but extremely rude email, not only to his friend, but to (4) .... in the company he worked for.

Other problematic emails are forwarded (5) .... purpose. Lawyer Richard Phillips emailed his secretary (6) .... her that she had spilt something on his trousers and asking her to pay the cleaning bill for the (7) .... of £4. This email, which was passed around many other law firms, was answered with a stinging reply by his secretary, which also (8) .... around the legal world. In the end Mr Phillips was so embarrassed that he left his job.

So, think carefully before you next click that 'send' button …

3 Read the **how to do it** box. Then read the text again carefully and for 1–8 decide which answer (A, B, C or D) best fits each gap.

how to do it

Read the text quickly, ignoring the gaps, to get the general meaning.

Read the text carefully, and for each gap, think of a possible answer before looking at the options.

Try each option in the gap before deciding.

0   A way
   (B) means
   C model
   D result

1   A mistaken
   B false
   C bad
   D wrong

2   A rather
   B other than
   C in place of
   D instead of

3   A to
   B at
   C into
   D up to

4   A anyone
   B everyone
   C no one
   D all

5   A for
   B on
   C to
   D in

6   A writing
   B saying
   C telling
   D replying

7   A sum
   B amount
   C money
   D quantity

8   A recycled
   B circled
   C circulated
   D cycled

Vocabulary

Phrasal verbs

1 Decide which verbs are more appropriate in these sentences – the phrasal verbs or the more formal equivalents.

a   Please note that candidates may not *leave out/ omit* more than two questions.

b   Did you read about that guy who stole loads of library books? They should *lock him up/ imprison him* when they get him.

c   Come on, Mum. *Speed up/Accelerate* a bit or we'll never get there!

d   Further to our recent telephone conversation, I am *sending back/returning* the faulty camera in question and *asking for/requesting* a full refund.

e   Hang on, I need to *work out/calculate* how much money this is going to cost me!

f   Guests are kindly requested to *get out of/vacate* their rooms by 11 a.m. on the day of departure.

2 Read sentences 1–4 below, then do the following.

a   Match each of the phrasal verbs in brackets with a verb it can replace in the sentence.

b   Rewrite each sentence using the phrasal verbs.

1   I'd love to discover why Jack rejected the offer of a free holiday with me, so try to raise the topic when you speak to him! (*bring up, find out, turn down*)

2   We departed early in the morning, but we encountered heavy traffic on the motorway, which really delayed us. (*hold up, run into, set off*)

3   Wait a minute. Are you saying that you submitted the application form without completing your name and address? (*fill in, hang on, send in*)

4   My brother didn't confess to breaking the window – instead he invented some story about two men throwing a brick then escaping on a motorbike. (*own up, make off, make up*)

Writing

Part 2 A review

1 Look at these verb phrases and discuss the questions below.

edit your profile	join groups	make online purchases
post messages	read message boards	search for friends
update your status	upload photos	visit chatrooms
write comments		

 a Which of these online activities do you do regularly? Which have you rarely or never done?

 b In your opinion, do social networking sites make it easier or more difficult for people to make and keep friends? Give reasons.

2 Discuss these questions in pairs.

 a Which websites do you visit regularly?

 b In your opinion, what makes a website easy or difficult to use?

 c How would you improve the websites you visit regularly?

3 Read the website review below and answer these questions.

 a What aspects of the website does the writer like and dislike?

 b What kind of people will like the website, according to the writer?

HOME | BLOG | REVIEWS

WEBSITE review: *gamenetter*

Gamenetter is a social networking site aimed at video game players. Launched less than a year ago, it already boasts in excess of four million users worldwide, according to its own publicity.

The graphics are eye-catching, with lots of animations and pop-up windows. This gives the site a young, dynamic look but sometimes at the expense of clarity. In particular, allowing users to choose their own fonts and backgrounds for their profiles makes some of the text almost illegible.

The site is quite difficult to navigate at first. Setting up and editing your profile is not as straightforward as on most sites. Finding your way around the members' area also takes some practice. Occasionally, pages take an unacceptable amount of time to load.

On the plus side, however, there are chatrooms and message boards where you can challenge other members to online games. There's also an online store and an advanced search facility for finding like-minded gamers in your area. All in all, although this website leaves a lot to be desired in terms of appearance and usability, its excellent features will guarantee its continued success among dedicated gamers.

4 Complete sentences a–g with these words.

cut	glance	hand	room
side	spot	way	

a At first ...., the site is rather plain with lots of white space, as if the designers were only interested in clarity.

b Being able to send a picture message to everyone in your group is a useful short .... that will prove popular with users.

c Unfortunately, the site has a serious weak ....: it does not allow users to upload video clips.

d Overall, there is considerable .... for improvement, despite some appealing aspects.

e The site is currently available only in English, but according to the developers a Japanese version is in ....

f Frustratingly, the number of high-definition video clips make navigation a bit on the slow ....

g The background images are spectacular, without getting in the ...., and the icons are cool and stylish.

5 Which sentences in 4 could be used to:

a give general information about a website?
b describe a website's appearance?
c comment on how easy a website is to use?
d discuss a website's features?
e give a general opinion of a website?

 how to do it

Divide your review into four paragraphs:

1 general information about the website
2 a description of the website's appearance
3 comments on ease of use (speed, navigation, etc.)
4 discussion of features (i.e. what the website offers users) and your overall judgement

6 Read the exam task below and the **how to do it** box. Then write a review (140–190 words) including language from this section.

You recently saw this notice in a magazine called *Teen Netwise*.

Website Reviews

Have you visited any new websites recently? Can you tell a good website from a bad one?

Write a review of a website focusing on its appearance, ease of use and features. Send it to *Teen Netwise* and we'll publish the best!

Write your review.

Review

1 Rewrite sentences a–g using another verb to replace *get*.

a I couldn't get the shop to give me a refund.

b Tom's very lucky – he never gets coughs or colds.

c I really don't get the point of what you're saying.

d The ship got smaller and smaller before disappearing over the horizon.

e What time did you get home last night?

f Sam got the highest possible score in his music exam.

g When did you get that digital camera?

2 Complete the phrasal verbs with *get* in sentences a–g.

a His father insisted that Robert did his homework before dinner. He couldn't get .... it.

b It really gets me .... when you don't do your share of the housework.

c My dad's getting .... He's nearly seventy.

d In the last lesson we got .... page 34 of the Student's Book.

e We got .... six packets of crisps while we were watching the film.

f Stop getting .... your brother. It isn't fair to criticize him like that all the time.

g The train got .... ten minutes late so I missed my connection.

3 Match phrasal verbs a–f with their more formal equivalents 1–6.

a work out   1 invent

b set off   2 confess

c turn down   3 accelerate

d make up   4 reject

e own up   5 calculate

f speed up   6 depart

4 Complete the sentences with an appropriate verb from 3.

a I can't .... the answers to any of these maths questions!

b We didn't want to go to the cinema, so we .... an excuse.

c In order to escape the earth's gravity, a rocket needs to .... to approximately 11 kilometres per second.

d We .... really early to avoid the rush-hour traffic.

e Jason .... my invitation to our house-warming party.

f Come on! .... ! Who put salt in my tea?

5 Complete these lines from website reviews with these words and phrases.

| according to | aimed | all | edit |
| first | look | plus | upload |

a *BargainTime* is a shopping site .... at the over-50s.

b The site has a plain, traditional .... which might put off younger users.

c At .... sight, the website is very colourful and appealing.

d On the .... side, it is easy to navigate.

e All in .... , there is considerable room for improvement.

f You can easily .... your profile and .... photos.

g .... Wikipedia, the website records around 40 million unique users a week.

A matter of taste

Lead in

1 ▶ 21 Listen to five people describing how to make a dish from their country. Match the speakers with the photos and say which countries you think the dishes are from.

Speaker	Photo
1	....
2	....
3	....
4	....
5	....

A

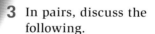

B

2 Imagine you are in a restaurant in your country with a foreign visitor. Choose two national dishes to recommend and describe them. Say

- if it's a savoury dish or a sweet dish
- when you eat it
- what the main ingredients are and how it's cooked.

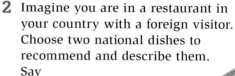

D

3 In pairs, discuss the following.

a Is it very important to you what you eat? What foods do you particularly enjoy eating?

b What foods do you dislike? What is it about them you don't like? Think about taste, smell, texture and appearance.

c Do you enjoy cooking? Why/ Why not?

C

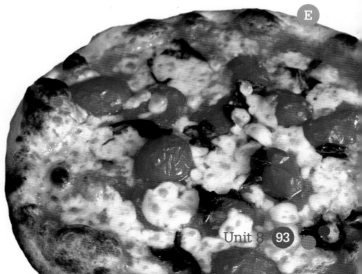

E

Reading

Part 6 Gapped text

1 What kind of restaurants do you prefer eating in? Why?

2 Read the text opposite quickly, ignoring the gaps, to find out what is unusual about the two restaurants described. Then explain what is happening in the photo at the bottom right of this page.

3 Read the text again carefully and the **how to do it** box, then match sentences A–G with gaps 1–6. There is one extra sentence.

A He, after all, was the one who brought us snail porridge and bacon ice-cream.

B They want their guests to concentrate solely on the food that is in front of them.

C The first does so by excluding other sensory input altogether.

D On the other hand, it must be a very strange experience for diners.

E The dish looks like a picture of the seashore.

F Then you are led to your table in the pitch-black dining room by a blind waiter.

G Some critics claim that diners will lose out on the social side of dining.

how to do it

Read the text quickly to get the general idea.

Look for links with grammar and vocabulary before and after each gap and in the sentences.

Fill the easiest gaps first.

Try the extra sentence in each gap again.

Read the text again, checking your answers.

4 Discuss the question in the final sentence of the text, giving reasons.

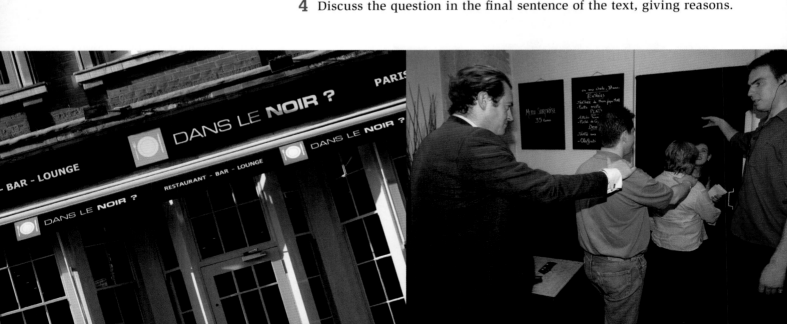

The Great Taste Sensation

WHY do we eat out in restaurants? Eating out is often about more than just the taste of the food. But for two restaurant owners in the south of England, this lack of focus is unacceptable.

5 **1** Interestingly, they set about achieving this in completely different ways.

Would you be happy to eat something if you couldn't see it? Edouard de Broglie, the restaurateur behind the London restaurant 'Dans le Noir', hopes so. He

10 believes that your sense of taste is intensified if you are not distracted by what you can see. 'Dans le Noir' is French for 'in the dark' and it is a blacked-out restaurant, where blind waiters and waitresses serve your food. **2** Others accept that the darkness brings

15 an added sense of intimacy. De Broglie, whose interest is in the sensory not the social aspects of dining, said, 'The preconception of what food tastes like because of how it looks is gone. All your other senses are abruptly awoken and you taste the food like you have never

20 tasted it before.'

When you arrive at the restaurant you can choose from the menu in the brightly-lit reception area. **3** You will have to feel for your cutlery, try to find the food on your plate, and try not to spill your wine! According

25 to Dr Charles Spence, an Oxford University lecturer in experimental psychology, everybody should try it. He said, 'We are visually dominant creatures driven by our eyes and anything you can do to change that is a worthwhile venture.'

Heston Blumenthal, chef and owner of the famous 30 restaurant 'The Fat Duck' near London, has long been renowned for his adventurous menus and experimental cooking. **4** But even his most extraordinary dishes will seem dull and ordinary compared with his latest creation of seafood served with an iPod. 35

No, diners will not be expected to eat the music player, but instead to listen to the noise of crashing waves as they eat. The creation, entitled 'Sound Of The Sea', is part of the tasting menu at the three-Michelin-starred restaurant. **5** It is presented on a glass-topped box containing sand 40 and seashells, and consists of what looks like sand but is in fact a mixture of fried breadcrumbs, fried baby eels and oil, topped with different kinds of seafood and three kinds of edible seaweed, all arranged beautifully. The final touch is the iPod, so that diners can listen to the sound of the 45 sea while they eat.

Blumenthal strongly believes that the sound of the waves intensifies the taste experience of eating seafood. 'I did a series of tests with Dr Charles Spence at Oxford University three years ago,' he said, 'which revealed that sound can 50 really enhance the sense of taste. We ate an oyster while listening to the sea and it tasted stronger and saltier, for example.'

Both of these restaurants seek to intensify the sensation of taste while you are eating. **6** The second does so by 55 adding to it. So which eating experience would appeal more to *your* senses?

Vocabulary

Food

1 Say whether these adjectives are positive, negative or neutral, depending on the context.

> bitter   chewy   crunchy   fatty   greasy   mild
> plain   rich   salty   spicy   stodgy   sweet
> tasteless   tasty   tender

2 Decide which adjectives from 1 you would use to describe these foods and drinks.

> curry   olives   ice-cream   fried chicken
> steak   boiled rice   coffee

3 Match the methods of cooking with pictures 1–7. Give an example of one kind of food that is often prepared in each way.

> fried   boiled   roast   grilled   barbecued
> baked   stewed

Grammar

Speculating about the present and past GR p170

1 Read sentences 1–6 and do the following.

  a Underline the modal verb in each of 1–6.

  b Match the meanings of the modal verbs with these phrases.
   - I'm sure it's true that …
   - It's possibly true that …
   - I'm sure it isn't true that …

  c Say which refer to the present, and which to the past.

1 That fish can't be cooked yet. It's only been under the grill for two minutes.

2 This meat is a bit dry and chewy. The chef must have overcooked it.

3 There were three tins of olives in the cupboard. We can't have eaten them all, can we?

4 Don't take the chicken out of the freezer yet. We might be eating out tonight if I can book a table.

5 You haven't eaten a thing since yesterday lunchtime. You must be starving.

6 I feel really ill. I think I might have eaten something that disagreed with me.

2 Rewrite sentences a–e using *must, might* or *can't*, as in the example.

Example   I'm sure you are joking.

You must be joking.

a   It's possible that he'll give you a ring this evening.

b   I'm sure Patricia isn't wearing her scarf. I saw it hanging on the hook on the back door.

c   I'm certain that James has got my mobile. I let him use it to call his sister this morning.

d   I'm sure that isn't Jim over there. His hair isn't as long as that.

e   I can possibly give you a hand with the cooking if I get home in good time.

3 Think of appropriate replies to these sentences using *must, might* or *can't*.

a   I feel hot and I've got a headache.

b   I've just seen a ghost.

c   I'm eating at a really expensive restaurant this evening.

d   My best friend has just been given the sack.

e   I had an argument with my best friend last night.

f   I've had enough. I'm going to live on a desert island.

4 Complete the sentences with the verbs in the box in the correct form. Use *must have, might have,* and *can't have.*

~~be~~	eat	invent	leave	spend
spill	stir	write down		

Example   Even the cat didn't eat the fish. It <u>must have been</u> bad.

a   His breath smells awful. He _____ a lot of garlic last night.

b   This sauce has gone all lumpy. I _____ it properly.

c   Beer _____ in Iran about 7,000 years ago, but nobody's quite sure.

d   What a fantastic spread. You _____ ages preparing all this food.

e   'Where are my keys?' 'You _____ them in the restaurant, or possibly in the car.'

f   I didn't order tomato soup. The waiter _____ the order correctly.

g   'There's a horrible stain on my new shirt. I _____ some food on it.'

5 Look at the photos. Speculate about them using *must (have), might (have)* and *can't (have),* as in the example.

Example   He must be hungry.

Listening

Part 3 Multiple matching

1 In pairs, tell each other about the last time you ate out. Say
- who you went with and why
- what you ate
- what the restaurant and food were like
- whether you'd recommend the restaurant

how to do it

Before you listen, read options A–H carefully.

As you listen, answer as many of the questions as you can.

When you listen again, concentrate on the answers you are least certain of.

2 ▶22 You will hear five people talking about a problem they had when eating out. Read the **How to do it** box, then match the speakers with the problems A–H. There are three extra letters.

Speaker 1	....
Speaker 2	....
Speaker 3	....
Speaker 4	....
Speaker 5	....

A ate in a different restaurant from the one they'd booked

B had to cancel their reservation because they were so late

C didn't mind waiting a while for a table

D ended up cooking at home

E booked a table but couldn't find the restaurant

F ended up having a takeaway

G had to wait a while for the food

H was unhappy at the way they were treated by the restaurant

3 Tell a partner about any bad experiences you've had when eating out. Think about
- booking a table
- finding a restaurant
- arrangements to meet
- food
- service

Speaking

Parts 3 and 4

1 Look at the photos below and match this description to one of the restaurants.

It looks very traditional and formal. I expect the food is dear, possibly overpriced. I expect it's quite quiet, too.

2 In pairs, take it in turns to say a sentence describing the other restaurant. Use the words below to help you.

boring	cramped	dear	exciting	formal
friendly	value for money	informal	lively
noisy	overpriced	quiet	romantic
traditional	trendy

3 ▶23 Listen to two people discussing where to eat. Do they manage to come to an agreement?

4 ▶23 Listen again and number sentences a–h in the order you hear them.

a Can't we go somewhere nicer? ....

b *Gianni's* is OK but it isn't very lively. ....

c I don't fancy an Indian. ....

d I expect the food's a bit basic. ....

e I'd prefer somewhere quieter. ....

f I'm not that keen on Chinese food. ....

g It looks very noisy. ....

h The service is terrible. ....

5 In pairs look at these restaurant signs. What do you imagine the restaurants are like? Choose one and talk about it using words from 2 and your own ideas. Your partner should guess which one you are talking about.

6 In pairs, look at the diagram and do the tasks below. Use words and phrases from 2 and 4.

Imagine you are planning a meal out with friends to celebrate the end of your exams. Discuss how suitable each of the restaurants shown might be and why.

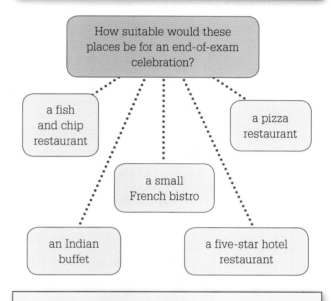

How suitable would these places be for an end-of-exam celebration?

- a fish and chip restaurant
- a pizza restaurant
- a small French bistro
- an Indian buffet
- a five-star hotel restaurant

Decide which restaurant to go to.

ROCKY'S FISH 'N' CHIPS
• EAT IN OR TAKE AWAY •

THE ROCHESTER
London's finest hotel restaurant

PAOLO'S PIZZA PARLOUR

MES AMIS
INTIMATE FRENCH BISTRO

BALTI BUFFET
All you can eat Indian cuisine

Use of English

Part 3 Word formation

●●● Adjective suffixes

We can add suffixes to nouns or verbs to make them into adjectives.
Sometimes the spelling changes.

-y	-ous
chew > chewy	mystery > mysterious
-al	**-ful**
music > musical	hope > hopeful
-able	**-less**
rely > reliable	use > useless

We can often use different suffixes with the same word to create
adjectives with different meanings:

taste: *tasty* – delicious *tasteful* – attractive *tasteless* – without taste; inappropriate

1 Read the information about adjective suffixes. Which suffix forms a negative adjective?

2 Work in pairs. In two minutes, think of as many adjectives as possible with the endings
in the box.

3 Complete sentences a–g with an appropriate adjective formed from the word in brackets.

Example   Tom's cousin is a .... singer. (fame)
                    Tom's cousin is a famous singer.

a   She may seem a bit cold and distant at times, but Cathy is a very kind and
        .... woman. (thought)
b   It was .... of Harry not to invite his best friend to his new girlfriend's party. (thought)
c   I first visited Madrid on a .... day in September. (rain)
d   They've opened a night shelter for .... people in our area. (home)
e   He's so .... about tennis that he plays it three times a week. (fanatic)
f   This coffee isn't great but it's .... if you're desperate! (drink)
g   Many medicines are .... if you take more than the recommended dose. (harm)

4 Read the text opposite, then complete each gap with a word formed from 1–8.

    0 say   5 tired
    1 harm   6 laugh
    2 sugar   7 health
    3 meet   8 absolute
    4 pleasure

5 Find four gaps in the text in 4 where you have to make an adjective from a noun.

6 Do you agree with the advice given in the text?

Eat, drink and be merry!

Or so the (0) _saying_ **goes**. But until recently, doctors have been telling us to do the opposite, warning us that overeating is (1) .... Now it seems that fatty or sweet, (2) .... foods can be good for us.

Recently, at a three-day (3) .... in Venice, a group of doctors, psychologists, and chemists discussed the idea that things that are (4) .... have a positive effect on our health and wellbeing. Guilt, stress, and (5) .... lead to illness. Love, (6) .... and pleasure, including eating things that are generally considered bad for you, keep our immune systems strong and therefore improve our health.

However, we mustn't eat too much (7) .... food, and when we do eat it, we must really enjoy it. There's (8) .... no point in eating a bar of chocolate and feeling guilty about it, because that creates a double negative – it's not healthy and has given you no enjoyment! Remember, eat, drink and be MERRY!

Vocabulary

●●● **Word** pairs

There are many word pairs that are joined by a conjunction. The order of the words is fixed.

bread and butter	wait and see

Sometimes the words in the pair are near synonyms.

fun and games	law and order

Sometimes the words in the pair are opposites.

take it or leave it	give and take

1 Read the information about word pairs. Make sure you understand the meaning of the examples, then match a–e with 1–5.

a	sick	1	sound
b	pick	2	tired
c	safe	3	choose
d	peace	4	pieces
e	bits	5	quiet

2 Say whether the word pairs in 1 are
- verb + verb
- noun + noun
- adjective + adjective

3 Complete word pairs a–e with opposites, then check your answers in a dictionary.

a more or ....
b back to ....
c sooner or ....
d now and ....
e ups and ....

4 Rewrite sentences a–g replacing the underlined phrases with pairs of words from 1 and 3.

a I've had enough of your complaining! Give it a rest, will you?
b Eventually Steve will realize his mistake.
c John spent his summer holiday travelling up the Amazon, but he's arrived home healthy and unharmed.
d As a child, I had to eat what I was given. I wasn't allowed to have only what I liked.
e The UK is approximately 1,200 kilometres long from north to south.
f We hardly ever eat out but occasionally we get a takeaway.
g 'Have you moved all that rubbish out of the spare room yet?' 'Nearly. There are just a few small things left.'

Writing

Part 2 A report

1 What facilities are or were available in your school?

2 Read the task and the report, ignoring the underlining. Decide whether the report

    a supports the idea

    b opposes the idea

    c recommends a different course of action.

> The director of your language school has put forward an idea to remove the only food and drinks machine. You have been asked to find out the views of your fellow students and write a report with your recommendation.

REPORT ON IDEA TO REMOVE FOOD AND DRINKS MACHINE

Introduction

The <u>aim</u> of this report is to <u>consider</u> the <u>pros and cons</u> of removing the food and drinks machine from the student common room, and to make a recommendation to the director of the school.

Advantages

There are some strong arguments <u>in favour of</u> removing the machine. It is felt that it:

- is old, ugly and noisy.
- takes up valuable space.
- sells only unhealthy foods, such as crisps, sweets and fizzy drinks.

Disadvantages

Removing the machine would also have <u>drawbacks</u>.

- A lot of students use it and would be unhappy if it were removed.
- The machine saves people valuable time as they do not have to go out and buy snacks at the local shops.

Conclusion

Although there are <u>convincing</u> arguments for removing the machine, I believe <u>on balance</u> that the disadvantages of doing so outweigh the advantages. However, I recommend that it is replaced with a smaller, more modern model that has a wider range of snacks, including some healthy ones.

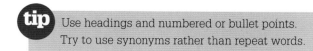

tip Use headings and numbered or bullet points.
Try to use synonyms rather than repeat words.

3 Under which heading does the writer do the following?

a   list the arguments against the idea

b   make a recommendation

c   state the aim of the report

d   list the arguments for the idea

4 Read the **tip** box, then match the words and phrases below with the synonyms underlined in the report.

a   advantages and disadvantages

b   strong

c   examine

d   disadvantages

e   for

f   purpose

g   after considering all the information

5 Read the task below, then divide sentences a–h into two groups: arguments for and arguments against the idea. Add any other arguments you can think of.

> The director of the school suggests closing the canteen and using the space for a student recreation room, with a TV and pool table. You have been asked to write a report on the advantages and disadvantages of this idea.

a   The canteen is underused.

b   The canteen food isn't very good.

c   The canteen food is cheap.

d   The canteen is very popular.

e   There's an excellent café opposite the school.

f   Students need a place to relax between and after lessons.

g   There's a TV in the café opposite the school.

h   Pool is popular among boys but not among girls.

6 Write a report of between 140 and 190 words. Divide your report into four sections, using the same headings as in the model report in 2. Use some of the arguments in 5.

Review

1 Choose the correct adjectives to complete a–e.

a This pork isn't very *stodgy/tender*. I should have cooked it for longer.

b I like nice green *crunchy/chewy* apples.

c These grapes are incredibly *rich/bitter*.

d 'How's your meal?' 'The bacon's OK but the fried eggs are rather *greasy/fatty*.'

e Crisps usually have a *mild/salty* taste.

2 Complete a–f using an adjective formed from the words in the box.

finance	forget	fury	penny	suit	wonder

a We saw a _____ play at the theatre last night.

b My dad was _____ when I stayed out all night.

c Grandad is getting more and more _____ as he gets older.

d He was _____ when he came to this country, but now he's a millionaire.

e The hotel doesn't have any rooms that are _____ for families.

f My brother works for a bank in the _____ district of Frankfurt.

3 Complete a–e with word pairs from the box using *and* or *or*.

give	later	less	more	safe	see
sooner	sound	take	wait		

a We were nearly involved in an accident on the motorway but we arrived home _____ .

b 'What's for pudding, Mum?'
'_____ . You haven't finished your first course yet.'

c The journey may take a long time, but we'll get there _____ .

d 'Is this the kind of thing you had in mind?' 'Yes, _____ .'

e If little Jimmy doesn't learn to _____ he won't make friends very easily.

4 For a–e complete the second sentence so that it has a similar meaning to the first sentence using the word given. Use between two and five words, including the word given. Do not change the word given.

a I'm sure you'll find your keys in the end.
turn
Your keys _____ later.

b It was very careless of you to spill coffee on the new rug.
careful
If you _____ you wouldn't have spilt coffee on the new rug.

c I've had enough of reality shows on TV.
tired
I'm sick _____ reality shows on TV.

d Linda thinks it's a good idea to install a new coffee machine.
favour
Linda is _____ a new coffee machine.

e This curry isn't spicy enough.
mild
This curry _____ .

5 Complete these lines from reports with the following words and phrases.

cons	convincing	drawback	examine
on balance	pros	purpose	

The .... of this report is to .... the .... and .... of the proposal to buy more computers for the school.

The most .... argument is that the computers are too slow for broadband Internet.

The only .... seems to be that there would be less money to spend on books in the coming year.

.... I think that the proposal is worth recommending.

Going to extremes 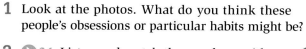 **9**

Lead in

1 Look at the photos. What do you think these people's obsessions or particular habits might be?

2 ▶24 Listen and match the speakers with sentences a–e.

a   I'm a terrible time-keeper.
b   I can never throw things away.
c   I'm a shopaholic.
d   I'm really untidy.
e   I'm obsessively well organized.

Speaker	Sentence
1	....
2	....
3	....
4	....
5	....

3 Discuss these questions.

a   Are the characteristics in 2 generally good or bad?
b   Do you have any particular habits (good or bad)?
c   How easy is it to learn new habits or stop bad ones?

Reading

Part 5 Multiple choice

1 Discuss whether you agree or disagree with the statement below. Give examples to support your opinion.

> You can't experience **real** excitement without taking risks.

2 The article opposite is about people who take risks. Read the text quickly and find the names of the two people in the photos.

3 Find these adjectives in the text and explain their meanings in the context in your own words.

  a   countless (l. 12)
  b   tiny (l. 20)
  c   inhospitable (l. 35)
  d   furious (l. 40)
  e   even (l. 46)
  f   major (l. 50)
  g   single-minded (l. 63)
  h   addictive (l. 66)

4 Read the text again carefully and for questions 1–6, choose the best answer (A, B, C or D).

  1   According to the text, most people would prefer to have
     A a comfortable life without risk.
     B occasional chances to test their endurance.
     C some experience of danger.
     D fewer unpleasant tasks in their lives.

  2   Kanchana Ketkeaw did not suffer serious injury from the scorpions because
     A they did not sting her.
     B scorpion stings are not very dangerous.
     C she did not allow many scorpions to touch her body.
     D her body has become used to the poison.

  3   The writer of the text believes that Kanchana Ketkeaw
     A is a bit mad.
     B was asked to perform her feat by her country.
     C did not perform her feat only for her country.
     D does not know why she performed her feat.

  4   Why is Lynne Cox particularly well suited to what she does?
     A Her style of swimming is similar to a seal's.
     B She likes swimming in outdoor pools.
     C She's rather fat.
     D Unusually, the fat below her skin has a regular thickness.

  5   Sir Ranulph Fiennes uses the memory of his father
     A to give him strength at difficult moments.
     B to remind him of the limits of human endurance.
     C to remind him that death is always a risk.
     D to help him make difficult decisions.

  6   Adventurers find that they cannot stop taking risks because
     A they have become famous for risk-taking.
     B their lives are less stable than other people's.
     C they love the feeling it produces.
     D they believe they can achieve the impossible.

5 Which of the three people in the article do you admire, if any? Why?

AGAINST ALL ODDS

Why do some people feel compelled to do the craziest things, while most of us are happy to sit on the sofa and watch their exploits on TV? Robin Styles ponders this question.

5 **Generally,** we love to watch someone's bravery and drama – a single person against the wilds of nature, testing their endurance beyond belief. And our pleasure is greater because we live in a comfortable world of central heating, gadgets and package holidays. We lead increasingly risk-
10 free lives, where the greatest test of endurance is getting to work through the rush hour. And most of us would prefer it to remain that way. However, there are countless ways to test the limits of your endurance, should you wish to do so, by attempting something unpleasant,
15 uncomfortable or just plain dangerous.

Thirty-year-old performance artist, Kanchana Ketkeaw, who spent 32 days and nights in a scorpion-filled room, said that she completed her amazing feat of endurance for her country, Thailand. The new world record holder
20 shared a tiny room for over a month with 3,400 deadly little friends, and was stung at least nine times! Fortunately she has worked with scorpions
25 for several years now and has developed some natural protection against their poison. Anyone else would be dead. To endure all that for her
30 country, which certainly didn't request it of her, must seem a bit mad to most people! There must be another reason.

American Lynne Cox swims in sub-zero temperatures through the planet's most inhospitable oceans wearing 35 only a swimsuit – for fun! According to Lynne, now in her fifties, there is always something driving her on. She just has to do it. As a nine-year-old child she was rather fat, and she used to swim in an outdoor pool with the local youth club. One day a furious storm blew up, but she 40 refused to get out of the pool. Something made her carry on. Then she realized that, as the water got colder and rougher, she was actually getting faster and warmer, and she was really enjoying it. At the age of 14 she broke her first endurance record, one of many more to come. Years 45 later, experts discovered that Lynne has a totally even layer of body fat, like a seal. She is perfectly made for doing what she does, it seems.

The famous British explorer, Sir Ranulph Fiennes, has led many major expeditions (and has lost several fingers) 50 in the extreme cold, including walking right round the Arctic Circle, which took three years! He has also led expeditions in the extreme heat, and discovered the Lost City of Ubar in the Omani desert. It seems that many adventurers spend their lives trying to live up to the 55 image of a parent. Sir Ranulph's father was Commander of a regiment in the British Army, and died just before his son was born. Fiennes has said, 'If I am getting weak, I find a very powerful way of squashing it is to know that my father would have definitely done it.' 60

Adventurers are clearly different from the rest of us. There is probably no such thing as a 'normal' adventurer. Unsurprisingly, risk-takers tend to be single-minded and unusually determined people who hate the stability and routine that most people prefer. They tend to take risks 65 for the sheer 'fun' of it. The excitement becomes addictive, and they want more and more of it. Ordinary life seems boring in comparison. The famous sailor, Sir Robin Knox-Johnston says: 'Humans have been taking risks since we evolved. If something is difficult, almost impossible 70 to achieve, then it is worth doing.' Well, obviously. Could someone please pass me the TV remote control?

Vocabulary

Compound adjectives

1 Decide whether compound adjectives a–h describe personality (P) or appearance (A).

- a bald-headed ....
- b bad-tempered ....
- c brown-eyed ....
- d curly-haired ....
- e easy-going ....
- f long-legged ....
- g rosy-cheeked ....
- h suntanned ....

2 For each of the pairs in a–d, use one of the words below to form compound adjectives.

> headed   hearted   minded   self

- a warm-............
  broken-............
- b absent-............
  broad-............
- c ....-centred
  ....-disciplined
- d big-............
  hard-............

3 Say which qualities in 2 are generally positive, negative or neutral.

4 Give examples of how someone with the qualities in 2 might behave.

5 Can you name any famous people (real or fictional) that you think have the characteristics in 1 or 2?

Grammar

Relative clauses GR p171–172

1 Read sentences 1–8 below then answer questions a–g about them.

1 What was the name of the English explorer *who walked to the South Pole in 1912*?

2 In 1911, *when he was 42 years old*, Captain Robert Scott organized an expedition to the South Pole.

3 There were 33 people in Scott's expedition, *which set out on 1st June 1910*.

4 The men *who Scott took with him* were mostly army or naval officers.

5 The Norwegian explorer Amundsen, *whose party arrived at the South Pole a month earlier than Scott*, returned home safely.

6 When Scott arrived at the South Pole, he found a tent and a letter, *which Amundsen had left there for him*.

7 Scott and his men all died before they could reach the supply depot, *where they had left food and spare clothing*.

8 Scott had taken horses instead of dogs with him, *which most people agree was a big mistake*.

a In which sentences is the relative pronoun the subject of the verb in the relative clause?

b In which sentences is the relative the object of the verb in the relative clause?

c In which sentence can we leave out the relative pronoun?

d In which sentences can we use *that* instead of *who* or *which*?

e Which type of clause has commas immediately before the relative pronoun?

f In which sentence can we replace *who* with the more formal *whom*?

g In which sentence does the relative refer to the whole of the main clause?

2 Join the pairs of sentences in a–e using *who* or *which*, adding commas where necessary and making any other changes.

Example   The plasma TV has broken. I only bought it last week.

The plasma TV, which I only bought last week, has broken.

a That's the man. He's going to buy our house.

b I gave my daughter twenty euros. She spent it immediately.

c I live in a village called South Milton. It's a mile from the sea.

d Where are the sausages? Mum bought them on Saturday.

e Daniel Craig plays James Bond in *Skyfall*. He also starred in the gangster film *Layer Cake*.

3 Complete the sentences with *who*, *which*, *when*, *where* or *whose*, adding commas where necessary.

Example   Harry is the guy _____ I met in Miyazaki _____ is a small town in Japan _____ we both taught English in the 1990s.

Harry is the guy *who* I met in Miyazaki, *which* is a small town in Japan *where* we both taught English in the 1990s.

a The shop _____ I usually get my groceries stays open until 10, _____ most other shops are shut.

b This chest of drawers _____ I inherited from my grandmother is 100 years old.

c Patricia is the girl _____ car we borrowed to go to that Spanish restaurant _____ they do great paella.

d Near my house is a park _____ there are some trees _____ my daughter loves climbing.

e The tall man _____ is standing over there is the cousin of the man _____ I introduced you to last night.

4 Look again at your answers to 3. Decide for each one

a if the relative pronoun could be omitted.

b if it would be possible to use *that* instead.

5 Correct the mistakes in a–e. Sometimes more than one answer is possible.

Example   Can you describe the man which you saw running out of the bank?

Can you describe the man *who* you saw running out of the bank?

a He's going to retire at 50, what I find surprising.

b Elvis Presley, that was probably the most famous pop star ever, died in 1977.

c Pam Fisher, who's older brother is a doctor, has also decided to study medicine.

d I got a letter this morning from my uncle Algernon who lives in Canada.

e The childminder looks after our children is ill today.

Listening

Part 2 Sentence completion

1 In pairs, tell each other about anything you collect now, or have collected in the past.

2 ▶25 You will hear a man called Alec Gardiner talking about the things he collects. Read the **how to do it** box, then listen and complete sentences 1–10.

how to do it

Before you listen, you have 45 seconds to read the 10 sentences.

If you miss an answer, don't worry. Move on to the next sentence.

When you listen again, concentrate on the answers that you missed the first time.

Don't leave answers blank – make a guess.

1 Alec isn't exactly _____ why he collects things.

2 Alec started collecting when he was _____ .

3 As a child Alec kept the things he collected in _____ .

4 Alec says it's a wonderful feeling when he completes a _____ of something.

5 Alec likes collecting cartoon figures because they look _____ and they amuse him.

6 It's possible to collect so many Mickey Mouse figures because Mickey is the _____ cartoon character.

7 Alec keeps most of his cartoon figures in the living room on small _____ .

8 Alec used to buy things at collectors' _____ and antique shops.

9 Alec doesn't like to leave the house for too long because he's afraid of _____ .

10 In order to complete a set of something, Alec sometimes has to pay out _____ hundred pounds.

3 ▶25 Complete Alec's sentences a–e with the adjectives below. Listen again and check, then explain the difference between the *-ed* form and the *-ing* form of the adjectives.

amazed/amazing bored/boring
interested/interesting pleased/pleasing
worried/worrying satisfied/satisfying

a I was never _____ as a child because there was always something new to collect.

b I became _____ in more things and started collecting them as well.

c The most _____ thing is when I find the last object to complete a set of something. That's really _____ .

d You'd be _____ where Mickey turns up!

e Everything in there is precious, and I'm _____ about burglaries.

4 In pairs, tell each other about
a something you are interested in.
b something you find boring.
c something you are pleased about.
d something you were amazed to find out.

Speaking

Part 2

1 Match these adjectives with photo 1 or photo 2. Say what each adjective could describe: the people, the venue, the event, the atmosphere, the clothes, etc.

> casual   colourful   crowded   excited   formal   grand
> imposing   relaxed   sophisticated   spacious

2 In pairs, brainstorm as many similarities and differences between the photos as you can and decide which are the most obvious. Use some of the phrases below to help you.

Similarities
- The most obvious similarity is that both photos show ....
- You can see .... in both photos.
- The room in photo 1 is .... Similarly, the room in photo 2 is ....

Differences
- The biggest difference between the photos is that photo 1 shows .... whereas photo 2 shows ....
- While photo 1 shows .... , photo 2 on the other hand ....
- The .... is/are completely different in the two photos.

3 In pairs, take turns to be A and B in the task below.

> **Student A:** Compare the photographs and say what you think the people are enjoying about being at these different parties.
>
> **Student B:** Say which party you would prefer to be at and why.

4 Discuss these questions.
a What kind of occasion do you think each party might be celebrating?
b What is your ideal kind of party? Talk about the venue, the atmosphere, etc.

Use of English

Part 4 Key word transformations

1 Read the **how to do it** box. Then look at the completed key word transformations in 1–4 and say which of these language areas is being tested in each.

| passives | phrasal verbs | relatives |
| comparatives | adjectives | modal verbs |

1 We didn't return to James' house until 11 p.m.
   got
   We finally <u>got back to</u> James' house at 11 p.m.
   language area ....

2 They lost the box containing all the exam papers.
   which
   They lost the box <u>which contained</u> all the exam papers.
   language area ....

3 Is Jason taller than Michael?
   as
   Is Michael <u>as tall as</u> Jason?
   language area ....

4 They always opened his letters before he received them.
   were
   His letters <u>were always opened</u> before he received them.
   language area ....

how to do it

- Decide what the key word replaces. Remember it could be part of a phrase.
- Read both sentences to check that they mean the same.
- Check the number of words you have written. Remember that contractions, e.g. *isn't*, count as two words.

2 Rewrite each sentence a–f keeping the same meaning. Use two to five words, including the word given.

a I haven't seen Harriet since February.
   time
   The last .... in February.

b It will be interesting to see if anybody can solve this problem.
   interested
   I .... to see if anybody can solve this problem.

c I'm sure Sam was there because he's in one of my photos.
   must
   Sam .... because he's in one of my photos.

d I won't tolerate his rude behaviour any more.
   put
   I .... his rude behaviour any more.

e This coffee isn't cool enough to drink.
   too
   This coffee .... drink.

f I haven't got enough money to buy that MP3 player.
   can't
   I .... buy that MP3 player.

Vocabulary

Body idioms

1 Label the parts of the body shown using these words.

ankle	calf	elbow	heel	hip
palm	shin	thigh	waist	wrist

2 Complete idioms a–h with these words, then match them with definitions 1–8.

arm	brains	eye	face	foot
hand	leg	tongue		

a keep an .... on someone/something

b twist someone's ....

c pull someone's ....

d put your .... in it

e be on the tip of your ....

f give someone a ....

g keep a straight ....

h pick someone's ....

1 persuade or force someone to do something

2 find out about something from someone who knows more about it than you

3 watch someone/something carefully

4 help someone

5 play a joke on someone by making them believe something that isn't true

6 say or do something wrong, foolish or embarrassing

7 be something almost remembered or recalled, but not quite

8 manage not to laugh or smile at something you find funny

3 Tell a partner about a situation when

a you couldn't keep a straight face.

b someone pulled your leg.

c you put your foot in it.

d you twisted someone's arm.

e you picked someone's brains.

f somebody gave you a hand.

1 .... 2 ....

3 ....

4 ....

5 ....

6 ....

7 ....

8 ....

9 .... 10 ....

Writing

Part 1 An essay

1 Read the task and model answer below. Answer the questions.

a What is the student's overall answer to the question in the essay title and where is it expressed?

b Does the essay cover points 1 and 2 from the notes in the task? Where?

c Which ideas in the essay are not mentioned in the notes?

In your English class you have been talking about space exploration. Now your English teacher has asked you to write an essay. Write an essay using *all* the notes and give reasons for your point of view.

Essay question

Should governments spend money on space exploration?

Notes

Things to write about

1 what can be learned from space exploration

2 what else the money could be used for

3 your own idea

SHOULD GOVERNMENTS SPEND MONEY ON SPACE EXPLORATION?

Since the middle of the twentieth century, governments have spent money on sending rockets and satellites into space to explore our solar system and beyond. But is it money well spent? Or should the money be put to use tackling problems closer to home?

Throughout the ages, humans have longed to understand the universe we live in. Space exploration is an important part of our efforts to push back the frontiers of knowledge. Furthermore, what we learn of other planets may one day prove essential for our survival, if this world becomes too crowded or too polluted to inhabit.

It cannot be denied that, in large parts of the world, there are people living in dire poverty. The millions spent on space exploration could certainly provide assistance for them in the short term. However, it could also be argued that scientific progress offers us the best long-term chance of solving their problems.

All things considered, I believe governments should continue to fund space exploration. Although the money could be spent in other ways, I think scientific progress benefits the whole human race.

2 Complete expressions a–f with these words, then check your answers by finding them in the essay in 1.

| long | offer | prove | provide | put | spend |

a to .... money (on doing something)

b to .... something to use (doing something)

c to .... to do something

d to .... essential (for something)

e to .... assistance (for somebody)

f to .... (somebody) the chance (of doing something)

3 Complete the language boxes with these expressions. Which ones are in the essay in 1?

Additionally, …
All in all, …
All things considered, …
Furthermore, …
In short, …
It cannot be denied that …
It is certainly true that …
Moreover, …
The fact is, …
What is more, …

●●● Introducing a key point

It is often said that …

●●● Reinforcing a point

In addition, …

●●● Summing up

In conclusion, …

4 Which of these features are you likely to find in the introduction to an essay? Which are in the introduction to the essay in 1? In which part of an essay are you likely to find the other features?

a the writer's personal opinion

b rhetorical questions linked to the essay title

c a brief reference to the history of the topic

d a definition or clarification of words used in the title

e a brief summing up of both sides of the argument

f a general statement about the topic

5 In pairs, read the task below. Then discuss what other idea or ideas you could add for point 3 in the notes.

In your English class you have been talking about explorers and their expeditions to the North and South Poles. Now your English teacher has asked you to write an essay. Write an essay using *all* the notes and give reasons for your point of view.

Essay question

Are polar expeditions a waste of time and money?

Notes

Things to write about

1 what can be learned from polar expeditions

2 what else the money could be used for

3 your own idea

6 Complete these sentences in an appropriate way for an introduction to the essay in 5.

a Humans have always been fascinated by the idea of …

b Even in today's world of global travel, polar expeditions are …

c Humans have always needed challenges, and polar expeditions …

d It is just over a hundred years since … South Pole.

e But is it really the case that …?

f But could the money …?

g But shouldn't we ask ourselves whether …?

7 Write an essay (140–190 words) in answer to the task in 5. Use at least one of your sentences from 6 in the introduction.

Review

1 Complete sentences a–g with compound adjectives.

a My brother is really absent-................ . He's always forgetting and losing things.

b 'You're looking very sun................ , George. Have you been on holiday?' 'Yes' I've just spent two weeks in the south of Italy.'

c Melissa was extremely fond of her cat, so she was ....-hearted when it died.

d Geoff goes on and on about getting the top mark in his exam. He's so big-................ !

e 'I didn't think our new football coach was ....-tempered.' 'He may seem easy-going to you but he gets angry at the slightest thing.'

f Sam is too ....-centred to talk to people he thinks are unimportant or not useful to him.

g Cathy finds ....-headed men attractive, maybe it's because her dad lost his hair at an early age.

2 Complete the idioms in sentences a–h with these parts of the body.

arm	brains	eye	face	foot
hand	leg	tongue		

a 'Would you like another piece of chocolate?' 'Oh, go on then. If you twist my ....'

b David really put his .... in it when he asked Samantha how Steve was getting on. They split up three months ago!

c 'I'm having problems with my PC. You know all about computers, don't you? Can I pick your .... ?'

d 'John told me that you were moving to New York.' 'New York! No, he was just pulling your ....'

e 'What's the French for 'lawn'? It'll come to me in a moment. It's on the tip of my ....'

f 'I've got to carry these chairs upstairs.' 'I'll give you a(n) ....'

g We couldn't keep a straight .... when the head teacher nodded off during the lesson.

h Can you keep a(n) .... on the children for me while I'm out?

3 Complete the text with the correct verbs below (a, b or c) in the -ing or -ed form.

Alicia Hempleman-Adams pulled off an (1) .... achievement by walking 200 miles across the Arctic wilderness of Baffin Island when she was only 15. Alicia faced (2) .... challenges as she crossed mountain peaks, glaciers and steep-sided fjords. Her father had travelled the same route himself and at first the prospect of his young daughter following in his footsteps was (3) .... Because of her age, he felt (4) .... that she would find it too (5) .... He was also (6) .... that she could get frost-bite. Alicia, however, was (7) .... that she could do it, and she was proved right. Though very (8) .... by the end, she was (9) .... to achieve her goal.

1	a	amaze	b	annoy	c	entertain
2	a	concern	b	terrify	c	bore
3	a	horrify	b	entertain	c	amuse
4	a	confuse	b	satisfy	c	worry
5	a	embarrass	b	excite	c	exhaust
6	a	interest	b	concern	c	amuse
7	a	convince	b	please	c	entertain
8	a	bore	b	tire	c	relax
9	a	thrill	b	confuse	c	encourage

All in the mind

Lead in

1 ▶26 Look at photos 1–6 and listen to the people introducing themselves. Try to remember their names and what they say, but don't make any notes.

2 Which of a–g are you likely to remember easily? What could make them easy or hard to remember?

- a a phone number
- b a tune
- c English vocabulary
- d the steps of a dance
- e the clothes that somebody was wearing on a certain occasion
- f how to get to a place you've only visited once
- g the date of a friend's birthday

3 Do the quiz below then turn to page 153 to find out what your answers say about your learning style.

What's your **learning style**?

1 When you spell a difficult word in English, do you
- A try to see the word in your head?
- B say the word, either aloud or in your head?
- C write the word down to find out what feels right?

2 When you chat socially with other people, do you
- A use as few words as possible?
- B enjoy talking and listening?
- C use your hands a lot?

3 When you are trying to concentrate, are you distracted most by
- A untidiness?
- B sounds?
- C movement?

4 When you meet somebody again, having met them only once before, are you most likely to
- A forget their name but remember their face and where you met?
- B remember their name and what you talked about, but forget where you met them?
- C remember best what you did together?

5 When you read for pleasure, do you prefer
- A descriptions?
- B dialogue?
- C action?

6 When you learn to do something new, do you prefer
- A seeing a demonstration and a picture?
- B listening to verbal instructions?
- C trying by yourself first?

7 When you're learning how to use new computer software, do you
- A try to find diagrams and charts?
- B ask help from someone who knows the software?
- C keep experimenting until you've learnt how to use it?

4 Turn to page 154 and do part 2 of the Memory Test in 1.

Reading

Part 6 Gapped text

1 Try to answer these questions without using a clock, calculator, ruler or any other device. Are they easy, difficult or impossible?

   a How wide is the door of the room you're in, to the nearest millimetre?

   b What is the time to the nearest second?

   c What day of the week was 1st June 1768?

   d What is 7,623 x 4,592?

2 Read the magazine article opposite quickly and find the name of

   a a film about a man who can do amazing calculations in his head.

   b a man who performed an amazing musical feat.

   c the scientist who thinks that we all have the potential to do these things.

Switch off your mind and become a genius

At the age of three, Daniel Tammet suffered an epileptic fit. Ever since then he has been obsessed with numbers and counting. Now an adult, he is a mathematical and linguistic genius who can recite pi to 22,514 decimal places and can learn to speak a language fluently
5 in a matter of days. Daniel is a 'savant': somebody who has specific, extraordinary abilities, but who is incapable of most everyday tasks. **1**

Unlike most savants, however, Tammet is a good communicator. **2** He explains that his mathematical feats do not involve 'thinking'. Instead, he visualizes the number in his head, as if he's watching a film. For Daniel,
10 numbers are not abstract, they are real and familiar, like friends.

Daniel had difficulty coming to terms with his condition until he saw an American film called *Rain Man*, which tells the story of another savant who can perform very complex mental arithmetic with astonishing speed and accuracy. **3** 'We shared so much,' says Daniel, 'our love of key
15 dates from history, for instance, and our love of books.'

Kim was born in 1951 with an unusually formed brain. Doctors predicted that Kim would never be able to lead a normal life, and it is true that as an adult he had to be looked after by his father. As a child, he couldn't
20 walk until he was four years old. **4** ☐ He could use a dictionary when he was three years old. By the age of four and a half, he had memorized the first eight volumes of an encyclopaedia. Since childhood, he read, and could recall in detail, about 7,600 books. He could
25 read two pages simultaneously (one with each eye) in about ten seconds and remember forever what he had read.

Savants are very rare: there are only about 25 alive in the world today. Their special abilities differ. The
30 blind American savant, Leslie Lemke, was able to play Tchaikovsky's Piano Concerto No 1 without hesitation after hearing it once, even though he had never had a piano lesson. **5** ☐ Other talents have included being able to measure exact distances with the naked eye
35 and knowing the exact time without looking at a clock.

Intriguingly, some scientists believe that we all have these kinds of amazing abilities hidden deep inside our brains, but that we lose them as we grow up. **6** ☐ This theory is supported by the fact that, very
40 occasionally, people acquire these abilities in adult life as the result of brain damage. Allan Snyder, director of the Australian Centre for the Mind, believes that we all might be able to release special skills by somehow 'switching off' the normal, conscious functions of
45 the mind. He conducts experiments on himself, firing strong magnetic waves into his head to see whether he can temporarily become a savant. Although finding volunteers for his experiments can be difficult, as Snyder admits, he believes that the possibilities are
50 very exciting. 'We are all potential geniuses,' he claims.

3 Read the article again carefully, then choose from the sentences A–G the one which fits each gap (1–6). There is one extra sentence.

A The British savant Stephen Wiltshire managed to draw a highly accurate picture of the London skyline after a single helicopter trip over the city.

B Savants are different: they don't develop normally and as a result they retain their special abilities.

C However, he always had extraordinary mental abilities.

D For example, he cannot drive a car or wire a plug, nor does he know his left from his right.

E They all have a similar ability to do amazing calculations in their head, like Raymond Babbitt.

F Then he got to meet Kim Peek, the real-life savant on whom the character in the movie is based.

G He can reflect on his own special abilities in a way that most savants cannot.

4 Find words or phrases in the article that mean

a easily and well (lines 3–5)
b very quickly and without mistakes (lines 11–14)
c at the same time (lines 24–27)
d immediately (lines 29–33)
e sometimes, but not very often (lines 39–41)
f for a short time (lines 45–47)

5 Which of the special abilities mentioned in the article would you most like to have? How would you use it?

Vocabulary

Mental activities

1 Match a–j with 1–10 to form definitions of the verbs in italics.

 a If you *suspect* something is true …
 b If you *consider* someone to be attractive …
 c If you *doubt* something that you've heard …
 d If you *recollect* an experience …
 e If you *contemplate* your future …
 f If you *analyse* a problem …
 g If you *memorize* a number …
 h If you can't *comprehend* something …
 i If somebody *reminds* you of another person …
 j If an idea *occurs* to you …

 1 you think about it in a logical way.
 2 you think it probably isn't true.
 3 you learn it so that you won't forget it.
 4 that is your opinion.
 5 they make you think of that other person.
 6 you think about it for quite a long time.
 7 it comes into your mind suddenly.
 8 you think it might be true but you aren't sure.
 9 you don't understand it.
 10 you think about it at a later date.

2 Choose the correct verbs in italics to complete a–e.

 a I often sit and *contemplate/recollect* the meaning of life, but I *doubt/suspect* I'll ever find any answers!
 b It *reminded/occurred* to me last night that I usually like people who *remind/recollect* me of my parents.
 c Until then, she had always *considered/ contemplated* him a very logical person who could *analyse/contemplate* any situation.
 d She says that she has *recollected/memorized* 10,000 telephone numbers, but I strongly *suspect/doubt* that she's lying.
 e I *recollect/memorize* seeing snow for the first time when I was three years old; I couldn't *consider/comprehend* what was happening.

Grammar

Comparatives and superlatives
GR p172–173

1 Read sentences 1–8 below. In pairs decide

 a which sentences contain comparatives and which contain superlatives.
 b which sentences you agree with and which you disagree with.

 1 Women communicate *far better than* men.
 2 *The more attractive* you are, *the easier* it is to make friends.
 3 *The funniest* comedian ever is Steve Martin.
 4 *The most intelligent* people are often *the least talkative*.
 5 *The more* you study a language, *the harder* it gets.
 6 Humans are becoming *more and more dependent* on machines.
 7 Teenagers don't work *as hard as* adults.
 8 People are usually *more attractive than* they think.

2 Rewrite sentences a–f, keeping the same meaning, but using another form of comparative.

 Example I'm worse at remembering faces than I am at remembering names.

   I'm not as good at remembering faces as I am at remembering names.

 a My best friend drives more slowly than I do.
 b The weather is cooler in the autumn.
 c Air tickets are getting less and less expensive.
 d In my opinion, this exercise isn't as easy as it looks.
 e This school isn't as big as I remember it.
 f Our local shops are further than we'd like them to be.

3 In pairs, make comparisons about the photos in 1–3 using the adjectives given or your own ideas.

 Example I don't think a footballer is as athletic as a ballerina.

   I don't agree. I think a footballer is more athletic, but far less graceful.

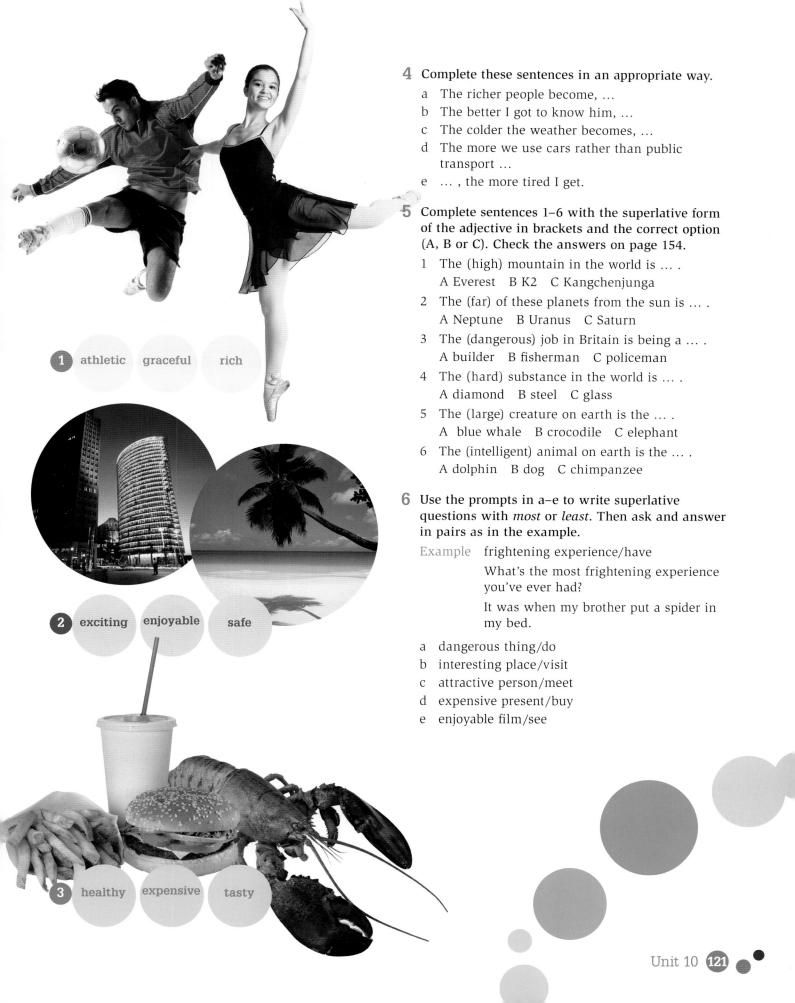

4 Complete these sentences in an appropriate way.

a The richer people become, ...

b The better I got to know him, ...

c The colder the weather becomes, ...

d The more we use cars rather than public transport ...

e ... , the more tired I get.

5 Complete sentences 1–6 with the superlative form of the adjective in brackets and the correct option (A, B or C). Check the answers on page 154.

1 The (high) mountain in the world is ... .
A Everest   B K2   C Kangchenjunga

2 The (far) of these planets from the sun is ... .
A Neptune   B Uranus   C Saturn

3 The (dangerous) job in Britain is being a ... .
A builder   B fisherman   C policeman

4 The (hard) substance in the world is ... .
A diamond   B steel   C glass

5 The (large) creature on earth is the ... .
A blue whale   B crocodile   C elephant

6 The (intelligent) animal on earth is the ... .
A dolphin   B dog   C chimpanzee

6 Use the prompts in a–e to write superlative questions with *most* or *least*. Then ask and answer in pairs as in the example.

Example   frightening experience/have

What's the most frightening experience you've ever had?

It was when my brother put a spider in my bed.

a dangerous thing/do

b interesting place/visit

c attractive person/meet

d expensive present/buy

e enjoyable film/see

1 athletic   graceful   rich

2 exciting   enjoyable   safe

3 healthy   expensive   tasty

Listening

Part 3 Multiple matching

1 Look at pictures 1–3. In your opinion, which one best conveys the feeling of being in a dream?

2 Discuss how dreams can be different from real life. Think about
   • people and places   • sequence of events   • feelings   • time

3 ▶27 You will hear five people talking about their dreams. Choose from the list A–H the things that each person dreams about. Use the letters only once. There are three extra letters.

A	things going wrong	Speaker 1	☐ **1**
B	animals	Speaker 2	☐ **2**
C	ordinary, everyday events	Speaker 3	☐ **3**
D	unconnected events	Speaker 4	☐ **4**
E	very recent events	Speaker 5	☐ **5**
F	strangers		
G	friends		
H	becoming rich		

4 ▶27 Complete the verb + preposition expressions that the speakers use. Then listen again and check your answers.

Speaker 1   I sometimes *make* _____ more interesting dreams.
Speaker 2   Things normally *work* _____ better in my dreams.
Speaker 3   I know I'm *messing* things _____ , but I can't help it.
Speaker 4   If I *came* _____ somebody from my dream, I'd be terrified.
Speaker 5   My brother is always *going* _____ about his dreams.

5 Replace each verb + preposition expression in 4 with a single verb.

6 Discuss these questions.

a   Do you analyse your dreams? What do you think some of them might mean?

b   Have any of your dreams ever come true?

Speaking

Part 2

1 Look at this list of sports and activities and answer the questions.

> long-distance running
> playing the piano
> sky-diving

a Why do people enjoy doing them?

b Which of the following qualities and abilities do people need to be successful at them?

agility	ambition	calmness
good concentration	confidence	courage
high energy	fitness	imagination
intelligence	patience	perseverance
sensitivity	stamina	strength

2 Match nouns a–h with photos 1 or 2. Brainstorm other nouns, verbs and adjectives you might need to describe the photos.

a	silence	e	piece
b	sail	f	wave
c	board	g	opponent
d	rocks	h	wind

3 Compare the photos and say how difficult it would be to excel at these activities. The phrases below and the **how to do it** box will help you.

●●● Comparing photos

> In the first photo … but in the second one …
> This picture … while on the other hand this one …
> In comparison to the first photo, this one …

how to do it

Describe each scene in general. Mention any obvious similarities or differences.

Say how they make you feel, or what they remind you of.

Describe what the people are doing and wearing.

Say how the people might be feeling and how you might feel in a similar situation.

4 In pairs, discuss which of the activities in the photos you'd enjoy more and why.

Use of English

Part 3 Word formation

●●● noun suffixes

We can add suffixes to verbs or adjectives to make nouns. Sometimes the spelling changes.

verb	→	noun
express	-(t)ion	expression
dominate		domination
manage	-ment	management
excite		excitement

adjective	→	noun
happy	-ness	happiness
weak		weakness
similar	-ity	similarity
popular		popularity

1 Add a suffix to each of the underlined words in a–g to make a noun that completes the second sentence.

Example   They <u>donated</u> a lot of money to Oxfam.
          They made a big <u>*donation*</u> to Oxfam.

a   My boss thinks it's very important to be <u>punctual</u>.
   My boss thinks .... is very important.

b   The police are <u>investigating</u> the crime.
   The police are carrying out an .... into the crime.

c   My secretary has resigned. I need to find someone to <u>replace</u> her.
   My secretary has resigned. I need to find a .... for her.

d   Unlike many superstars, she's well known for being <u>polite</u>.
   Unlike many superstars, she's well known for her ....

e   My brother is very <u>sensitive</u> to other people's feelings.
   My brother shows a great deal of .... to other people's feelings.

f   Do you <u>enjoy</u> watching reality TV shows?
   Do you get a lot of .... from watching reality TV shows?

g   Mick is <u>responsible</u> for organizing the Christmas party.
   Mick has .... for organizing the Christmas party.

Are geniuses born or made?

It is a common (0) *belief* that geniuses are different from ordinary people from birth. However, according to psychologist Professor Michael Howe, the secret of genius is hard work!

Professor Howe also believes that nearly all geniuses have the (1) ...... to concentrate for long periods of time. 'What makes geniuses (2) ...... is their long-term (3) ...... ,' he explains. 'They have a clear idea of their goal and pursue it with total (4) .... They make an exceptional effort and so their (5) ...... are exceptional.'

Throughout history, the (6) ...... composers in the world have often been child prodigies. However, even the most exceptionally able still took at least ten years of hard study to become a major composer.

It would be untrue to suggest that every genius begins as a child prodigy. Many (7) ...... talented adults – including Charles Darwin – were unexceptional in their youth. And what's more, many child prodigies do not go on to achieve anything (8) ...... as adults.

2 Read the text opposite, ignoring the gaps, and say whether a–c are true or false according to the text.

a Michael Howe believes that all geniuses are naturally clever.

b Even the best composers had to work hard to become great.

c All geniuses are very clever as children.

3 Complete the gaps in the text with words formed from 1–8 as shown.

Example   believe → *noun*
            belief

1 able → *noun*
2 difference → *adjective*
3 commit → *noun*
4 dedicate → *noun*
5 achieve → *noun*
6 great → *superlative form*
7 high → *adverb*
8 significance → *adjective*

Vocabulary

Expressions with *mind*

1 Look at expressions a–l and say in which ones *mind* is a verb, and in which a noun.

a mind your own business	g spring to mind
b Do you mind if …	h take your mind off something
c I don't mind + noun or *–ing*	i be bored out of your mind
d change your mind	j be in two minds about something
e make up your mind	k bear something in mind
f mind your head	l Would you mind + *–ing*

2 Use expressions from 1 in the correct form to complete what the people are saying or thinking in 1–4.

1 I'm _____
   _____ .

2 I hope you haven't _____
   _____ ?

3 Would you _____
   _____ ?

4 This film will _____
   _____ our problems.

3 Rewrite these sentences using an expression with *mind* from 1.

a As she watched the plane land, she suddenly remembered her own first experience of air travel.

b I can't decide which restaurant to go to this evening.

c Please could you open the door for me?

d My dad is happy to give us a lift into town.

e I don't want advice about my personal life. Please don't interfere.

f Is it all right if I give my friend your phone number?

Writing

Part 2 A letter

1 Read the task below and Raquel's letter. In which paragraph does she:
  a   say what else she is sending with the letter?
  b   say how good her English is, and how she'd like to improve it?
  c   give details of her qualifications?
  d   say where she saw the advertisement and why she is writing?

> You saw this advertisement in a newspaper and wish to apply for a place on a Diploma course. Write a letter of application to the Admissions Director of the college.
>
> ## GREENFIELD COLLEGE
>
> We offer post-graduate courses in English Literature at three levels: Diploma, MA and PhD. Courses start on 15th September and 15th January.
>
> Send your application letter to the Admissions Director, Kay Jordan, giving details of:
> - which course you are interested in
> - your qualifications and relevant experience
> - why you wish to study with us

Dear Ms Jordan,

I am writing in response to your advertisement in the Daily News for the Post-Graduate Diploma in English Literature. I want to apply for a place on the course that starts on 15th September.

I am 22 years old and have just done a degree in English Language and Literature at Madrid University, which I passed with Distinction. While at university I specialized in 19th-century literature. I have visited Britain a few times and went to summer language schools in Brighton and Oxford. I can read and write English very well.

I would now very much like to increase my knowledge of 20th-century literature. I am particularly keen to continue my studies in Britain in order to improve my speaking and listening skills.

Here's my CV with lots of information about my qualifications and work experience. I look forward to getting a reply.

Yours sincerely

Raquel Gonzalez

2 Raquel starts the letter with *Dear Ms Jordan* and finishes with *Yours sincerely*. How would she have started and finished the letter if she hadn't known the name of the recipient?

3 Find seven words or phrases in Raquel's letter which you could replace with words and phrases a–g to make it more formal.

a completed
b I enclose
c attended
d on a number of occasions
e hearing from you
f I would like to
g full details of

4 Match a–f with 1–6 to form sentences appropriate for a formal letter.

a I look forward to hearing from you
b As for my qualifications,
c I would be grateful if you could
d I should like to apply for
e I have two years' experience of
f I am available

1 … I have a degree in English.
2 … working in hotels.
3 … send me details of the syllabus.
4 … at your earliest convenience.
5 … for interview from 1st March.
6 … the post of receptionist.

5 Read the task, then write a letter of application (140–190 words). Follow the advice in the **how to do it** box.

> You saw this advertisement online and wish to apply for a place on a Cambridge Advanced course. Write a letter of application to the Admissions Director of the college.
>
> ### NORTH MIDLANDS COLLEGE
>
> We offer full- and part-time EFL courses that prepare students for the Cambridge First, Advanced and Proficiency exams:
>
> Our courses are usually oversubscribed, so apply early to avoid disappointment, clearly stating:
>
> - which course you are interested in
> - why you wish to study with us
> - any other relevant information about yourself
>
> Send your application letter to the Admissions Director, EFL.

how to do it

Read the task carefully and underline any words which tell you what information you need to include.

Begin by saying why you are writing.

Do not include addresses or the date.

Make sure your letter is organized into paragraphs.

Check your letter for length (140–190 words) and register.

tip Write one paragraph for each main idea. Don't write more than four paragraphs.

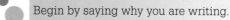

Review

1
Rewrite sentences a–i using the verbs in the box in the correct form, and making any other necessary changes to the sentences.

~~suspect~~	consider	memorize	remind
analyse	contemplate	occur	
comprehend	doubt	recollect	

Example
I've always thought that he didn't like me.
I've always suspected that he didn't like me.

a John makes me think of a friend I had at school.

b I don't think we will win the World Cup.

c In my opinion, he's very impolite.

d For homework my daughter had to learn a Shakespeare poem by heart.

e He's thinking carefully about resigning and looking for another job.

f We need to think logically about the results of the experiment.

g Can you remember exactly what he said?

h I suddenly thought of the answer in the bath.

i It's difficult to understand why she wants a divorce.

2
Form the part of speech shown in brackets from the words in a–h.

a astonish (noun)   e illegality (adjective)

b discussion (verb)   f sad (noun)

c inform (noun)   g carelessness (adjective)

d excitement (verb)   h similar (noun)

3
Use the correct form of words in 2 to complete these sentences.

a Liam and I had a long _____ about the advantages and disadvantages of living abroad.

b It was very _____ of David to lose the house keys.

c The police rang to _____ me that they'd caught the man who stole my car.

d Harry bears a striking _____ to his brother. It's sometimes difficult to tell them apart.

e In Britain it's _____ to sell cigarettes to people under 18.

f It was with great _____ that doctors announced the death of the much-loved president.

g Mark is incredibly forgetful. It would _____ me if he remembered his mother's birthday.

h The news that a circus was coming to town caused great _____ among the children.

4
Complete the text below using words formed from the base words in 1–8.

0	regular	3	difficult	6	participate
1	invite	4	sincere	7	equal
2	arrange	5	commit	8	sense

Why do we over-commit?

Most people **(0)** *regularly* over-commit. How often do we agree to meet friends, accept **(1)** _____, or offer to help a family member, only to realize that in making the **(2)** _____ we've been too generous with our time? Psychologists believe that we 'over-commit' because we have **(3)** _____ judging how much time there is available. We fill our diaries with things to do, **(4)** _____ believing that we'll have more time in the future than we have in the present. Of course, when tomorrow turns into today, we discover that we are too busy to fulfil all of the **(5)** _____ that we've made. The nature of time deceives us and we 'forget' about how things fill our days and compete for our time. Nearly all the **(6)** _____ in a survey believed that they would have more free time next month than now. When questioned a month later, they were surprised to find that they were **(7)** _____ busy. So next time you are invited to three parties in the same week, try to think ahead and consider whether it would be more **(8)** _____ to be less generous with your time.

Man and machine ¹¹

Lead in

1 Look at the photos of these things that we generally no longer use, and discuss these questions.

   a What were they used for?

   b What has replaced them?

   c Is the replacement better and, if so, in what way?

   d Did the older version have any advantages?

2 Which machines and gadgets that we currently use might become obsolete in the next few years? Why? What might replace them?

3 Do you think that boys and girls are equally interested in technology? Give reasons and examples.

Reading

Part 5 Multiple choice

1 How much time do you spend using these every day? Work out the average amount for each one, and compare answers with a partner. Do you think you spend too much time on any of them?

mobile phone	MP3 player	computer
	TV	

2 Read the text about children and technology, and say which of these statements is true, according to the text.

a On the whole, if used wisely, technology has more positive effects on children than negative ones.

b The positive and negative effects of technology on children are fairly equally balanced.

c The negative effects of technology on children are so bad that they outweigh any benefits.

3 Read the text again carefully, and for questions 1–6, choose the answer (A, B, C or D) which you thinks fits best, according to the text.

1 The US survey showed that

A every child spends over seven hours with gadgets.

B children spend more time on gadgets than ever before.

C most children use two gadgets at one time.

D American children spend more time with gadgets than other children.

2 According to the text, technology

A can help children develop mentally and physically.

B is the best tool for teaching children in school.

C is used by children principally for entertainment and fun.

D encourages children to work harder.

3 According to the text, what is another important advantage that computer skills give children?

A They help them to use social networking sites.

B They help with future employment.

C They make them better at talking.

D They make them more confident with people.

THE GADGET GENERATION

Children today would find it hard to imagine life without mobile phones, iPods, computer games and the Internet, and there are very few who aren't technically literate and skilled at using them.
5 Technology has advanced rapidly, particularly over the last decade, and gadgets and gismos will have an ever-increasing influence on children's lives. A survey of young people between the ages of eight and 18 in America showed that the average time children spend
10 using electronic gadgets has risen dramatically to around seven hours and 38 minutes a day. And some are consuming up to ten hours' electronic content a day, because they use more than one gadget at the same time.

15 Technology has without question improved the quality of children's lives. Children's television can be informative as well as entertaining, and in schools, computers are increasingly used as an aid to learning. Educational software frequently offers children the
20 chance to work together, take turns, discuss and solve problems, and all computer games help to improve motor skills and hand–eye co-ordination. Computers and the Internet offer children a sense of empowerment and provide them with the tools
25 and information needed to solve problems or find things out. Texting, emailing and blogging all drive children to be more experimental with the written word. A recent British survey showed that children who use technology are much more confident about
30 their writing skills. Technology also has a social role. Over 25% of British eight- to 11-year-olds who have a computer are members of an online social network like Facebook or Bebo. They make new friends and chat online, and consider this important, although

35 it can also have downsides. Furthermore, good
    computer skills are essential in today's job market,
    so the more confident children are with computers,
    the greater the advantage they will have when
    looking for a job.

40 Despite these considerable advantages, there is a
    widely held opinion that technology makes children
    lazy. While this isn't technically true, it can reduce
    or replace the opportunity for physical activity for
    some children. But is there an even darker side? Dr
45 Susan Greenfield believes that spending too long in
    cyberspace can actually alter the chemistry of the
    brain. As some children spend between six to nine
    hours daily staring at a screen, she thinks that their
    minds are developing differently. The more we play
50 games, the more we are focused on the process
    and the thrill of attaining the goal. When we win at
    something, a chemical called dopamine is released
    in the brain, which makes you feel happy and so
    becomes addictive. What does not count here is the
55 meaning and content – what does the game mean?
    Who are the characters in the game and why are
    they there? This is another level of understanding
    and reasoning that the brain needs and which is
    omitted in many computer games. Dr Greenfield is
60 concerned that if we don't do enough of the right
    type of thinking, our brains could become less able
    to function on all levels.

    Doctors also feel that the safe, ordered, two-
    dimensional computer world does not help children
65 operate in the messy, emotional, three-dimensional
    real world. Dealing with people through face-to-
    face conversations, activities and challenges, helps
    children to develop their own sense of self and
    identity. Computer games cannot help children
70 with everyday reality and can actually hinder their
    ability to deal with it.

    The message from psychologists seems to be clear.
    While banning computer games is clearly not an
    option, too much of anything is not a good thing.
75 But how much is too much and who decides?
    Psychologists say that two hours of gadget time a
    day is more than enough, but does that include
    homework, listening to music and emails to
    friends, for example? Is it up to parents, schools,
80 or the government? And what do young people
    themselves think?

4   How does Dr Greenfield feel about computer
    games?
    A She thinks they stop children exercising.
    B She thinks they are harmless fun.
    C She thinks they are potentially dangerous.
    D She thinks they are good, because they
       produce a useful chemical.

5   According to some doctors, computer games can
    A give children a false sense of reality.
    B help children understand the real world.
    C prevent children from having emotions.
    D help children deal with other people.

6   According to the text, the advice from
    psychologists is that children
    A can spend more time on gadgets, if it
       involves listening to music.
    B shouldn't do their homework on a computer.
    C should stop playing computer games
       altogether.
    D should never spend longer than a couple of
       hours a day with gadgets.

4 Match a–f with 1–6 to make verb–noun
   collocations. Then check your answers by finding
   them in the text.

   a use   1 turns
   b solve   2 new friends
   c take   3 a gadget
   d improve   4 a goal
   e make   5 a problem
   f attain   6 hand–eye co-ordination

5 Which of the points in the text do you agree or
   disagree with? Why?

Vocabulary

Gadgets and their parts

1 Read the advertisement below, then complete gaps 1–5 with these words.

| battery life | Internet access | ringtones | wireless | text |

4G NOKSUNG 4470

Chat to friends, ¹_____ them, or send picture messages with Noksung's latest 4G mobile.

- With ²_____ you can send and receive emails on your phone.
- Over 50 ³_____ to choose from – from a simple bell to a clip from a Top 20 single.
- The keypad is easy to use and has voice-activated dialling.
- Great ⁴_____ – you can get at least 80 hours of use.
- Make and receive calls while you are on the move using the ⁵_____ headset.
- Includes high-resolution digital camera.

2 Write an advertisement for this MP3 player. Use the advert in 1 as a model, and make it sound as attractive as possible.

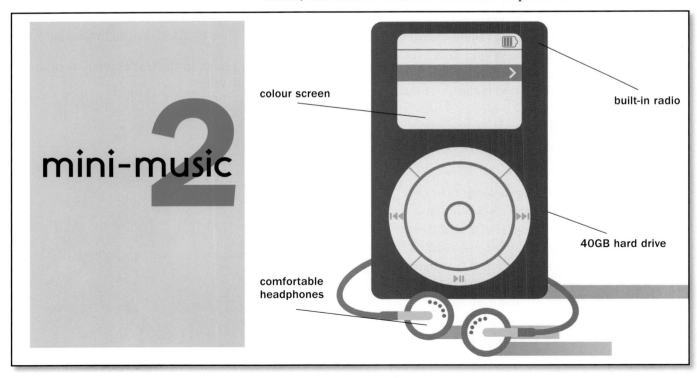

mini-music 2

colour screen

built-in radio

40GB hard drive

comfortable headphones

Grammar

Conditionals GR p174–175

1 Correct the mistakes in the underlined clauses in a–d and name the type of conditional (zero, 1st, 2nd or 3rd).

   a <u>If I would win the lottery</u>, I'd buy an enormous plasma TV.

   b If you give me a blank CD, <u>I burn the album onto it for you</u>.

   c <u>If you'll press this key</u>, it sends the text message.

   d <u>If I knew it was illegal</u>, I wouldn't have downloaded all those songs.

2 In pairs, decide if future events a–f are probable or improbable for your partner. Then, depending on your decision, write a question for each one using the first or second conditional.

   Example   go out this evening

           Improbable – Where would you go if you went out this evening?

           Probable – Where will you go if you go out this evening?

   a win the lottery

   b go to the cinema at the weekend

   c visit the UK this summer

   d surf the Internet at the weekend

   e lose your mobile phone

   f not have any homework this evening

3 In the same pairs, ask and answer the questions you wrote in 2.

4 Write sentences using the third conditional as in the example.

   Example   I missed the bus so I was late for my class.

           If I hadn't missed the bus, I wouldn't have been late for my class.

   a I bought a new MP3 player because I lost my old one.

   b I didn't know you liked opera, so I didn't buy you a ticket.

   c The burglar got in because I forgot to shut the window.

   d Carl didn't buy the computer because it was so expensive.

   e I couldn't find your number so I couldn't phone you.

5 Read mixed conditional sentences 1–4 and answer questions a–d below.

   1 If Jane didn't have a cold, she'd go swimming with Tom.

   2 If Jane didn't have a cold, she'd have gone swimming with Tom.

   3 If Josh hadn't spent all his money, he'd have gone out with his friends.

   4 If Josh hadn't spent all his money, he'd go out with his friends.

   a Does Jane have a cold in sentence 1, sentence 2 or both?

   b Has Tom already gone swimming in sentence 1, sentence 2 or both?

   c Has Josh spent all his money in sentence 3, sentence 4 or both?

   d Have his friends gone out in sentence 3, sentence 4 or both?

6 Complete sentences a–f with mixed conditionals.

   Example   Harry didn't go to the party because he's getting up early tomorrow.

           Harry would have gone to the party if he weren't getting up early tomorrow.

   a We have to walk to school because the car has broken down.

        _____ if the car hadn't broken down.

   b I won't speak to him because he was so rude to me. I would speak to him _____ .

   c I'm not interested in how this mobile works, so I didn't read the manual.

        If I'd been interested in how this mobile works, _____ .

   d You didn't listen to the instructions so you don't know what to do.

        _____ , you'd know what to do.

   e I'm annoyed because he borrowed my laptop without asking me first.

        _____ if he hadn't borrowed my laptop without asking.

   f The sea isn't very warm so we didn't go swimming.

        _____ we'd have gone swimming.

7 Complete these sentences in an appropriate way. Try to include some mixed conditionals.

   a If you show me how to turn on this laptop …

   b I'd use the Internet more often if …

   c If I'd known you were coming, …

   d I might have bought a motorbike if …

   e I'd have been amazed if …

Listening

Part 4 Multiple choice

1 Look at the photos and discuss these questions.

a Who do you think invented each one, a man or a woman? Why?

b Why do you think there were more male than female inventors in the past?

2 You are going to listen to a radio programme about inventors. First, read questions 1–7, but not the options, and decide which are the key words in the questions.

1 Why did Dr Franklin research female inventors?

A to prove to her colleagues that they existed

B to inspire girls to study science subjects

C to find out how many inventions they were responsible for

2 Why aren't there more women inventors in history?

A It wasn't an acceptable thing for a woman to do.

B Women didn't want to seem clever, even if they were.

C Very few women studied science.

3 Why were inventions often in the husband's name?

A The husband wanted to take the credit for his wife's ideas.

B Women couldn't afford to pay for patents.

C Wives did not have any right to ownership.

4 Lady Ada Lovelace didn't patent her invention because

A society didn't approve of women doing such things.

B she wasn't accepted as a lady.

C she wasn't of the right social class.

5 Josephine Cochrane became an inventor because

A she spent a lot of time at home.

B she didn't like washing up.

C her staff were careless.

6 Mary Anderson's invention became an obligatory safety feature

A for all vehicles in cold climates.

B for vehicles of all kinds.

C for all trams and buses.

7 Emily Canham's invention changed car headlights for the better by making them

A interfere less with other drivers.

B light up the road more brightly.

C shine to the side, not straight ahead.

3 ▶28 Now listen and choose the best answer, A, B or C, for questions 1–7 in 2.

4 Think about your answers to 1. Are you surprised by any of the information you heard?

Speaking

Parts 3 and 4

1 Identify the gadgets in the pictures. Then make a sentence for each one as in the example.

Example If we didn't have TV remote controls, we'd have to get up every time we wanted to change channels or adjust the volume.

2 ▶29 Listen to two students talking about some of the gadgets shown, and answer the following.

a Which gadgets do they decide are the most useful?

b Do you agree with their opinions?

3 ▶29 Listen again and say which of the expressions in the language box they use.

●●● Agreeing

Yes, I agree (with you).
I couldn't agree more.
So do I./Neither do I.
That's right/true.

●●● Disagreeing

I see what you mean, but …
That may be true, but …
Don't you think that … ?
That's a good point, but I …

4 In pairs, do the task below, using the phrases in 3 and the tip box to help you.

Discuss why each of the gadgets shown is useful, and how life would be different without it.

How would life be different without these gadgets?

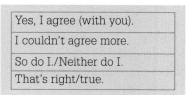
a smartphone   headphones   a laptop

a hairdryer   a radio

Decide which two gadgets would be most difficult to live without and why.

tip You can use these phrases for starting a Part 3 discussion:
Let's talk about … first.
We could start by talking about …
You can use these phrases for bringing a discussion to a close:
I think we need to make a decision.
Shall we try to come to an agreement?

5 Discuss these Part 4 questions.

a Do gadgets always make our lives easier?

b Can you think of a gadget which is completely unnecessary? Why is it unnecessary?

c Do you think we rely too much on computers?

d Do computers and gadgets make us antisocial?

Use of English

Part 2 Open cloze

1 Look at these dictionary entries then complete the gaps in sentences a–c.

ban 0–ᴡ /bæn/ *verb, noun*
- *verb* (-nn-) **1** 0–ᴡ ~ sth to decide or say officially that sth is not allowed **SYN** prohibit: *Chemical weapons are banned internationally.* **2** 0–ᴡ [usually passive] to order sb not to do sth, go somewhere, etc, especially officially: ~ **sb from sth** *He was banned from the meeting.* ◇ ~ **sb from doing sth** *She's been banned from leaving Greece while the allegations are investigated.* ◇ (BrE) *He was banned from driving for six months.*
- *noun* 0–ᴡ ~ **(on sth)** an official rule that says that sth is not allowed: *There is to be a total ban on smoking in the office.* ◇ *to* **impose/lift a ban**

re·spon·sible 0–ᴡ /rɪ'spɒnsəbl; *NAmE* -'spɑːn-/ *adj.*
▸ HAVING JOB/DUTY **1** 0–ᴡ having the job or duty of doing sth or taking care of sb/sth, so that you may be blamed if sth goes wrong: ~ **(for doing sth)** *Mike is responsible for designing the entire project.* ◇ ~ **(for sb/sth)** *Even where parents no longer live together, they each continue to be responsible for their children.*

spend 0–ᴡ /spend/ *verb, noun*
- *verb* (**spent, spent** /spent/) **1** 0–ᴡ [T, I] to give money to pay for goods, services, etc: ~ **sth** *I've spent all my money already.* ◇ ~ **sth on sth/on doing sth** *She spent £100 on a new dress.* ◇ ~ **(sth doing sth)** *The company has spent thousands of pounds updating their computer systems.* ◇ *I just can't seem to stop spending.*

Oxford Advanced Learner's Dictionary, 8th edition

a Some pressure groups have proposed a ban .... genetic engineering.

b Who is responsible .... organizing the trip to the science museum?

c Cathy spends a lot of money .... computer games.

2 Complete sentences a–g with these prepositions, then check your answers in a dictionary.

> for   on   to   with

a In the future we will rely .... robots to do menial tasks.

b There's something wrong .... this DVD player. I can't get it to record.

c Jack Kilby won a Nobel prize in 2000 for his contribution .... computer science.

d My brother has applied .... a job with IBM.

e There's a strong demand .... 4G mobile phones this Christmas.

f Scientists are trying to develop robots that are similar .... humans.

g You can use this software on a Mac, but it isn't compatible .... Windows.

3 Read the text opposite, then complete gaps 1–8 with one word each.

4 In which gaps in 3 did you need to add

a a preposition after a verb?

b a preposition after an adjective?

c a preposition after a noun?

WORLD CUP FOR ROBOTS

This week has seen (0) _the_ largest ever display of footballing skills – by robots. RoboCup, the World Cup in robotic football, has been taking place at an American university, with teams (1) _____ robots from all around the world participating.

The contestants in the Humanoid League are similar (2) _____ children in size, while those competing (3) _____ the Nano-Cup are (4) _____ small that a microscope is needed to see them. Compared to their human equivalents, robotic footballers (5) _____ many advantages: they can keep playing all day, they don't talk back, and if they ask for more money, you can simply take out their batteries.

Experts are confident that in less (6) _____ 50 years' time, football-playing robots capable of taking on a human side will have (7) _____ created. And the technology developed in order (8) _____ make RoboCup possible will be used after the World Cup for more important things such as search and rescue missions.

Vocabulary

Compound nouns

1 Read the compound nouns in the box, then answer questions a and b.

> Internet access   mobile phone
> search engine   artificial intelligence
> instant messaging

  a Which of them are formed from two nouns?
  b Which of them are formed from an adjective and a noun?

2 Complete a–e with compound nouns from 1.

  a *Google* is the most popular _____ on the Internet.
  b My teenage daughter sits at her computer all day using _____ to chat with her friends.
  c It's illegal to use a _____ while you're driving, unless you have hands-free equipment.
  d You can get _____ through any number of Internet service providers.
  e Scientists researching _____ have developed computers that can understand human speech.

3 Read the **tip** box, then form compound nouns for a–f using these words. Check your answers and spelling in a dictionary.

> board   lap   text   life
> screen   site

  a key_____   d computer_____
  b web_____   e _____top
  c battery_____   f _____message

tip Some compound nouns are written as a single word, some as two words, and some with a hyphen. Check in your dictionary if you aren't sure.

Writing

Part 1 An essay

1 **Read the task and model answer below. Answer these questions.**

a   How do mobile phones improve personal safety, according to the writer?

b   Can you think of any ways in which mobile phones could make people less safe?

c   Why is always being contactable not a good thing, according to the writer?

d   Can you think of any ways in which always being contactable is a good thing? Does the writer mention any?

> In your English class you have been talking about mobile phones. Now your English teacher has asked you to write an essay. Write an essay using *all* the notes and give reasons for your point of view.
>
> **Essay question**
>
> Would the world be better or worse without mobile phones?
>
> **Notes**
>
> Things to write about
>
> 1 personal safety
>
> 2 always being contactable
>
> 3 your own idea

WOULD THE WORLD BE BETTER OR WORSE WITHOUT MOBILE PHONES?

Fifty years ago, mobile phones did not exist; today, there are almost as many mobile phones in the world as there are people. But imagine they had never been invented. Would our lives be better or worse as a result?

Being able to make calls wherever you are is certainly convenient and sometimes makes you safer. For instance, what would you do if your car broke down on a remote country road and you did not have a mobile phone to call for assistance? Additionally, many parents are more willing to let their children go out alone or with friends because they know they can always phone or text if they are in trouble.

On the other hand, having a mobile phone with you day and night can make it impossible to relax. For example, these days, many people are contacted by their office even when they're at home or on holiday. Furthermore, smartphones mean they may also have to deal with emails.

Overall, I think mobile phones have brought us more advantages than disadvantages. However, I also believe that it's a good idea to switch them off sometimes.

2 Find these things in the essay in 1:

a   a brief reference to the past

b   a rhetorical question related to the title

c   two different ways of introducing an example

d   two different ways of introducing a point which reinforces the point before

e   three ways of introducing a contrast

f   a phrase which introduces a conclusion

3 In pairs, read the task below. What is your initial answer to the essay question? Give a reason.

> In your English class you have been talking about technology in schools. Now your English teacher has asked you to write an essay. Write an essay using *all* the notes and give reasons for your point of view.
>
> **Essay question**
>
> Would a school without computers of any kind be a better or worse place to learn?
>
> **Notes**
>
> Things to write about
>
> 1 how computers are used in schools
>
> 2 other kinds of activities in school
>
> 3 your own idea

4 In pairs, ask and answer questions a–h. Does thinking about these questions make any difference to your initial answer in 3?

a   Do young people spend too much of their free time using computers (tablets, smartphones, etc.)?

b   Are sports and physical education an important part of school life?

c   Are many teenagers more knowledgeable about computers than their teachers?

d   Is the Internet a safe place for children to explore?

e   Is learning to write by hand still an important part of education?

f   Do children learn better if they can choose their own activities in school?

g   Are printed books old-fashioned and out of place in today's classroom?

h   How often would schools need to replace their computers (tablets, etc.) in order to stay up to date?

5 Plan your essay by making notes in the chart below. Remember that you must cover points 1–3 in the task.

Paragraph 1: Introduction (Could include reference to the past and / or a rhetorical question.)
Paragraph 2: One side of the argument (Should be whichever side of the argument you support. Give examples.)
Paragraph 3: The other side of the argument (Include at least one point for the opposing side. Give examples.)
Paragraph 4: Conclusion (Sum up the arguments and restate your position.)

6 Write your essay in 140–190 words in an appropriate style. Use your plan from 5.

Review

1 Read the definitions in a–d and complete the words they define.

a something that helps you use your mobile phone without having to hold it to your ear

w............ headset

b a way of sending very quick text messages between computers

i............ m............

c to send a written message between mobile phones

t............

d the sound a mobile phone makes when someone is calling you

r............

2 Make complete sentences by matching a–h with 1–8.

a More and more people are getting interested
b The high demand
c I am responsible
d You can't rely
e There's a total ban
f My sister has applied
g George seems to be completely unable to learn
h The huge increase in air travel has made a significant contribution

1 on Mark to keep a secret.
2 for a place to study medicine at university.
3 to global warming.
4 from his mistakes.
5 in technology.
6 for oil has pushed prices up.
7 on smoking in our office.
8 for keeping the website updated.

3 Complete sentences a–e with compound nouns. One part of each compound (either the first or the second) is given in brackets.

a I've got a wireless .... on my computer. (key)
b If you leave your MP3 player switched on, you may shorten its .... (life)
c .... is an area of computer science that focuses on creating machines that can think. (intelligence)
d My dad takes his .... with him every morning so that he can work on the train. (lap)
e If you're planning to sell goods on the Internet, you need a well-designed .... (web)

4 Complete the sentences with a word or phrase that expresses contrast. There may be more than one possible answer.

a .... he's very wealthy, he's very careful with his money.
b iPods are fantastic gadgets. They are, ... , quite a bit more expensive than most MP3 players.
c John doesn't have a mobile phone, ... his sister Kate has three!
d I do like Peter, ... I have to say, he can be very moody and difficult.
e Scientists have built computers that can understand speech. .... , I don't think they will ever develop a machine that can actually think.
f I thought I'd lost my mobile. .... , it turned up in my wife's handbag.

5 Choose the correct words and phrases.

1 Young people generally feel more comfortable with computers than older people. *For instance, / However,* teachers often ask students to help them with technology in the classroom.

2 Teenagers spend too much time playing computer games. *On the other hand, / Additionally,* computers are useful for online research.

3 Computers are increasingly being used in language teaching. *However, / Overall,* I don't think they will replace books in the near future.

4 Tablets break easily if you drop them. *For example, / Furthermore,* they are still quite expensive.

5 *Overall, / For example,* I believe computers bring more advantages than disadvantages.

Make a difference

Lead in

1 Match these social issues with photos 1–5, and describe what each photo shows.

    street crime   vandalism   homelessness   graffiti   begging

2 Are any of these social issues a problem where you live? What other similar problems can you think of?

3 Discuss the impact of the issues from 2. Think about their effect locally and nationally, then decide on an order, from most serious to least serious.

4 Discuss how individuals and governments could tackle these problems. Try to agree on one practical measure for each issue.

Reading

Part 7 Multiple matching

1 Read the text opposite quickly, then match the photos with sections A–F. Which section does not have a photo?

2 Read the text again carefully, then for questions 1–10, choose from the people or groups A–F.

Which person or group

1. has very well-known supporters?
2. is more likely to repeat the stunt if people get annoyed?
3. was not staging a genuine protest?
4. uses food as a weapon?
5. got into trouble with the law?
6. used an unusual costume to gain media attention?
7. used a government building in their protest?
8. has performed similar stunts in various countries?
9. was very unpopular with animal rights groups?
10. has successfully disrupted public transport?

3 Complete the verb + noun collocations in a–g, then check your answers by finding them in the text.

| bring   cause   earn   become   make   raise   have |

a to .... front-page news (l. 4)
b to .... a dislike for somebody (l. 11–12)
c to .... a target (l. 20)
d to .... (public) awareness (l. 24)
e to .... something to someone's attention (l. 29–30)
f to .... a scandal (l. 36)
g to .... yourself a nickname (l. 49)

4 Giving reasons, say which of the stunts described was, in your opinion

a the most unusual
b the most physically demanding
c for the best cause.

PERFORMING PROTESTS

When American protestors threw 40,000 kilos of tea into Boston Harbour in 1773 to protest against unfair taxes, they made front-page news around
5 the world. Although the 'Boston Tea Party' was not particularly successful in political terms, it demonstrated the power of the publicity stunt. In today's society of 24-hour news, a good stunt is an even more valuable weapon
10 for campaigners.

A Noël Godin

Noël Godin is a Belgian writer, critic, and actor who has
a particular dislike for public figures whom he considers
to be self-important. His unusual form of protest against
these people is to push a large cream pie into their face.
15 His most famous victim is probably Bill Gates, whom he
'cream pied' in 1998, making news headlines around the
world. If his victim reacts badly to the stunt, Godin does
it again at a later date. The French philosopher Bernard-
Henri Lévy got so angry with Godin that he has now
20 become a regular target!

B PETA

PETA (People for the Ethical Treatment of Animals) is
an animal rights organization with several high-profile
supporters, including Hollywood star Pamela Anderson. In
2005, to raise public awareness of its campaign against
25 fast-food chain KFC, a PETA volunteer dressed as a
chicken and, sitting in a wheelchair, repeatedly crossed
the road outside a KFC franchise in South Carolina, USA.
Though the protest did not put customers off, it achieved
its wider objective: it featured on TV news, bringing the
30 issue to the public's attention.

C Mark McGowan

British performance artist Mark McGowan has a track
record of eye-catching stunts. In 2003, to protest against
university tuition fees, he used his nose to push a peanut
along the pavement for 10 kilometres, finishing outside
35 the Prime Minister's residence in Downing Street. In 2007,
he caused a scandal by eating a swan as a protest against
the monarchy. According to an old law, all swans in the UK
are the property of the queen, and eating one is a crime.
However, it was not the police who objected: McGowan
40 received death threats from animal rights activists!

D Alain Robert

In 2003, Alain Robert climbed the 180m TotalFinaElf
skyscraper in Paris, with his bare hands. He made the
ascent without ropes or safety equipment, wearing an anti-
war T-shirt. A crowd of onlookers cheered when, after 45
45 minutes, he safely reached the top of the building, where he
was arrested by waiting police. Since then, he has climbed
some of the tallest buildings in the world, including the
Petronas Twin Towers in Malaysia – twice. No wonder he
has earned himself the nickname 'the French Spiderman'.

E Plane Stupid

50 Plane Stupid is an environmental group whose chief goals
are to put an end to airport expansion and to stop short-
haul flights. They have occupied a number of airports,
preventing flights from departing and arriving, as well
the headquarters of low-cost airlines such as EasyJet.
55 Their most eye-catching protest was in 2005, when five
activists climbed onto the roof of the Houses of Parliament
in London and unfurled two long banners, with slogans
calling for the scrapping of plans to build a third runway at
London's Heathrow Airport.

F Electronic Arts

60 In 2009, a group of 13 angry protestors gathered outside
a Convention Centre in Los Angeles to demonstrate against
'Dante's Inferno', a new video game produced by a company
called Electronic Arts, on religious grounds. They handed
out leaflets which included a link to a website. What
65 baffled some journalists was that the website seemed
to be promoting the game rather than condemning it. It
subsequently emerged that the 'protestors' had in fact been
hired by Electronic Arts themselves in order to mount an
elaborate publicity stunt.

Vocabulary

Achievement and success

1 Complete phrases a–e with the words below.

> achieve ambition manage succeed target

a fulfil/realize a/an ....
b reach a/an ....
c .... success
d .... to do something
e .... in doing something

2 Rewrite sentences a–d using the verb in brackets in the correct form.

a The protestors were not successful in changing the government's policy. (manage)
b Sophia Coppola was successful in the film industry at a young age. (achieve)
c Despite winning *Pop Idol*, she was unable to make a career in music. (succeed)
d Last year, students from our school cycled around Britain to raise money for Oxfam, and successfully raised a figure of £60,000. (reach)

3 Complete sentences a–e with the words below.

> achievable achievement realization
> success successful

a Winning an Olympic gold medal was the .... of a lifelong ambition.
b Failure is not an option; we expect ....
c The first .... non-stop flight across the Atlantic was made in 1919.
d Discovering the tomb of Tutankhamen was Howard Carter's greatest ....
e Learning to drive in a month is difficult, but ....

4 In pairs, tell each other about
- an ambition that you have realized.
- an ambition that you have not yet fulfilled.
- something that you hope to achieve within the next year.

Grammar

Causative verbs: *have, make, let* and *get* GR p175

1 Complete gaps 1–5 in the text with the correct forms of *have, let, get* or *make*.

Students back hair protest

Students at a college have staged a protest at the treatment of a fellow student. The row began when Gavin Trent, 17, [1]_____ his hair dyed with the colours of his favourite football team. At first, the school would not [2]_____ Gavin attend classes with his new hairstyle, claiming that it might [3]_____ fans of other teams become aggressive. After discussions, Gavin [4]_____ the school to change its mind and allow him back into school, but he was [5]_____ to wear a hat during lessons.

2 Complete sentences a–g with the verbs in the box. Use the correct form of *have* + part participle.

> cut decorate deliver develop
> service steal take

a I must .... my car .... The engine's making an odd sound.
b We .... our living-room .... last week. It looks fantastic with its fresh coat of paint.
c Many celebrities hate .... their photos .... by press photographers.
d When did you last .... your hair .... ?
e We .... three newspapers .... on Sundays.
f One advantage of a digital camera is that you don't need to .... the pictures ....
g If you leave your mobile phone visible in the car you're likely to .... it ....

3 Look at the pictures and say what work the owners of this house have had done. Write sentences as in the example using the verbs below.

build	make	put on	put in
finish	remove		

Example   They've had the roof put on.

4 Complete sentences a–f using *make*, in active or passive form, and an appropriate verb.

a   The film had a very sad ending that .... me ....

b   When I was younger I .... 10 minutes of violin practice every evening by my parents.

c   In the nineteenth century many British children .... long hours in factories.

d   I think I've made myself clear. Don't .... me .... myself.

e   That song always .... me .... of college. I used to listen to it all the time as a student.

f   At the surgery Sam .... for over an hour to see the doctor.

5 In pairs, talk about what your parents made you do or let you do when you were younger, as in the example. Use the phrases below and your own ideas.

- stay up late
- tidy your bedroom
- learn a musical instrument
- wash your own clothes
- surf the Internet
- have a computer in your bedroom
- watch anything you liked on TV

Example   Did your parents let you stay up late?

Not very late. I had to go to bed before seven until I was about 10 years old.

Did they make you tidy your bedroom?

Yes, they did, but not very often.

6 Say what you would do in each of these situations using *have, get, make* and *let.*

a   You are at a party and somebody spills orange juice on your new jacket.

b   Your best friend asks you to lend them a lot of money.

c   You see a group of teenagers in the street painting graffiti on a wall.

d   You have ordered some books on the Internet but they haven't arrived two weeks later.

e   Your neighbours' son keeps on kicking his ball into your garden.

f   You see a young woman shoplifting.

Listening

Part 2 Sentence completion

1 Read the quotations below. Do you agree or disagree with them? What do they tell you about some people's opinion of teenagers?

> Teenagers complain there's nothing to do, then stay out all night doing it.

> Little children, headache; big children, heartache.
> (Italian proverb)

> A boy becomes an adult three years before his parents think he does, and about two years after he thinks he does.

> Too many of today's children have straight teeth and crooked morals.

2 ▶30 You will hear council leader Jane Newton talking about a new way of controlling teenagers. Listen and complete sentences 1–10.

1 Councillor Jane Newton is giving a press conference inside the ....

2 She claims that vandals are responsible for more than .... pounds of damage a year.

3 Most of the vandalism in the town centre happens after .... and before 2 a.m.

4 The Mosquito doesn't affect .... because the noise is too high-pitched.

5 The first Mosquito will be installed in the

....

6 There are plans to install ten devices before

....

7 According to Jane Newton, ... per cent of vandalism is committed by teenagers.

8 Evidence from other .... suggests that the Mosquito does reduce crime.

9 She acknowledges that the Mosquito has already been banned in both .... and

....

10 She is confident of the Mosquito's .... despite recent research.

3 Do you think the Mosquito is a good or bad idea? Give reasons.

Speaking

Part 2

1 Match these words and phrases to photos 1 and 2.

> enclosure   freedom   man-made
> natural habitat   protected
> social group   solitary

tip Begin by making factual statements about the photos, including the most obvious similarities and differences. Then move on to comments which involve opinion or speculation.

2 Read the **tip** box, then decide which of a–g are factual, and which convey an opinion or speculation.

  a Photo 1 shows a solitary lion whereas photo 2 shows a group of lions.

  b I would imagine that the lion in photo 1 is quite bored.

  c The lion in photo 1 is in a zoo or safari park.

  d The lion in photo 1 probably has to cope with crowds of noisy visitors every day.

  e It's likely that the lions in photo 2 are more exposed to dangers.

  f The lion in photo 1 looks slightly depressed, in my view.

  g Photo 2 shows a group of lions in their natural environment.

3 In pairs, take turns to be A and B in the task below.

> **Student A:** Compare the photographs and say which place offers the better life for the lions, in your opinion.
>
> **Student B:** Say which place you would prefer to visit and why.

4 Say whether you agree or disagree with these statements. Give reasons.

  a It's cruel to keep animals in zoos.

  b Zoos help to save animals from extinction.

  c It doesn't matter if animal species become extinct. It's natural.

Use of English

Part 1 Multiple-choice cloze

1 Find the adjectives in italics in a–h in a dictionary and say whether one or both are possible in the sentences.

a Most of the information in that article is *false/untrue*.

b In the past, most people over the age of 50 had *false/untrue* teeth.

c The campsite is next to a *broad/wide* river.

d This leaflet will give you a *broad/wide* idea of the services we offer.

e He refused to discuss his divorce, saying it was a *personal/private* matter.

f Stories are usually more convincing when they're written from *personal/private* experience.

g The Chrysler Building is one of the *highest/tallest* buildings in New York.

h He poured the lemonade into a *high/tall* glass.

2 Read the text opposite, ignoring the gaps, and say whether sentences a–c about Daryl Hannah are true or false.

a She wants people to try 'green living' and thinks they will like it.

b She rarely talks about environmental issues because she dislikes confrontation.

c She makes videos about environmental issues but is not committed to them in her personal life.

3 Read the text again carefully and for 1–8 decide which answer (A, B, C or D) best fits each gap.

0	A arrives	B pulls	C reaches	D stops
1	A single	B moment	C moment's	D second
2	A scene	B picture	C view	D animation
3	A private	B personal	C personable	D separate
4	A contained	B followed	C added	D included
5	A for	B of	C to	D in
6	A making	B bringing	C having	D letting
7	A possible	B available	C ready	D easy
8	A do	B have	C give	D make

Green living

A Chevrolet (0) __*pulls*__ into a filling station and out steps Hollywood star Daryl Hannah. She fills up. Then she pours herself a glass of the green fuel, straight from the pump, and drinks it without a (1) _____ hesitation.

This attention-grabbing (2) _____ appears on Hannah's video blog. The blog, which features a new segment every week, reveals Hannah's (3) _____ experience of the latest in green living. Topics have (4) _____ environmentally-friendly buildings, vegan diet and biodiesel – one of Hannah's favourite issues.

Best known for her roles in films like *Blade Runner*, *Splash* and *Kill Bill*, Hannah has a long-standing commitment (5) _____ environmental living. But she's only recently started (6) _____ her green lifestyle to the attention of the public.

'People have to know that there are options (7) _____ to us today,' she said. 'There is another way, and it is practical and applicable now.'

Hannah's focus on solutions reaches people in a way that protest and confrontation can't. All she wants is for people to (8) _____ it a try.

Vocabulary

Compound adjectives

1 Match a–h with 1–8 to form compound adjectives.

a	eye-	1	quenching
b	labour-	2	catching
c	thirst-	3	saving
d	record-	4	warming
e	time-	5	watering
f	heart	6	consuming
g	mouth-	7	eating
h	meat-	8	breaking

2 Complete sentences a–h with compound adjectives from 1.

a Tyrannosaurus rex was a .... dinosaur whereas most dinosaurs were herbivores and ate plants.

b .... devices like washing machines and dishwashers have made life much easier.

c I don't think people will notice such a small advertisement – we need something more ....

d Fizzy drinks aren't as .... as water.

e She ran the last lap of the race in just 45 seconds – a .... achievement.

f Picking grapes by hand is very .... so the job is done by machines in many vineyards.

g There was a .... story on the news last night about a teenager who dived into a river and pulled a little girl to safety.

h This book contains hundreds of .... recipes. I highly recommend it.

3 Rewrite sentences a–e replacing the underlined phrases with compound adjectives, as in the example.

Example   He used to be a layabout, <u>who ate chocolate</u> and <u>watched TV</u>.

He used to be a chocolate-eating, TV-watching layabout.

a Newspapers always put headlines <u>that will grab people's attention</u> on the front page.

b He's always coming up with interesting ideas <u>to make money</u>.

c My uncle runs a company <u>that cleans windows</u>.

d In Nicaragua, Jinotega and Matagalpa are the largest areas <u>where they grow coffee</u>.

e The film <u>which won an award</u> is being shown on TV tonight.

Writing

Part 2 An article

1 Read the exam task below, then number the paragraphs in the article in the correct order. Say which words helped you.

2 Say which of 1–9 are
   a usually used in formal writing
   b usually used in informal writing
   c used in both formal and informal writing.

   1 not only … but also
   2 furthermore
   3 in addition
   4 on top of that
   5 what's more
   6 to make matters worse
   7 moreover
   8 as well as
   9 besides

3 Find five of the phrases in 2 in the article.

THREE STEPS
TO A BETTER ENVIRONMENT

How could the environment be improved in your town or village? Tell us your ideas for three changes that you think should be made.

We will publish the most interesting articles next month.

☐ First, I would have the multi-storey car park in the town centre demolished. Not only is it a very ugly building, but it also attracts criminals, especially after dark. Moreover, removing the car park would make people use public transport for coming into town.

☐ To sum up, if you visited Monkton, I'm sure you'd agree that these simple changes would make it a much more attractive town, as well as improving the quality of life of its inhabitants.

☐ Thirdly, I would ban lorries from driving through the town centre. They cause a lot of noise and pollution and what's more, they put people off cycling, because cyclists are afraid they will get knocked off their bikes.

☐ We would all like to make our towns and villages more pleasant places to live and work in. If I could make three changes to my hometown of Monkton, this is what I would do.

☐ Secondly, I would have the area around the lake cleaned up. At the moment, the banks are covered with litter. In addition, I would get the council to install some litter bins and erect some picnic tables.

4 Correct the underlined mistakes in a–e.

a Besides <u>to ban</u> cars from the centre, I'd have the roads resurfaced.

b Cars cause a lot of pollution as well as <u>they are</u> noisy.

c Not only <u>there are</u> not enough buses but they are old and dirty.

d <u>Moreover</u> is the town hall old, it's also ugly.

e In addition to <u>clean up</u> the park I'd have a children's playground installed.

5 Read the **tip** box, then find examples of how the writer has attempted to involve the reader.

tip Involve your readers by addressing them directly, and by using the personal pronouns *I*, *we* and *you*.

6 Imagine you have seen the announcement in 1 in a magazine called *Green Issues*. Work in pairs and decide on three areas for change, using the ideas below to help you.

air quality   noise   recycling
public transport   buildings and roads
facilities   parks and public spaces
shops   trees and plants

7 For each of the areas you chose in 6, write two sentences about how things could be improved. Try to use each of these grammatical structures at least once.

a have something done

b get someone to do something

c make something + adjective

d make someone do something

e would/wouldn't let someone do something

Example   I'd make people pick up their litter, or pay a fine.

8 Write your answer to the task in 1 in 140–190 words.

Review

1 Complete a–d using these verbs in the correct form.

manage   reach   realize   succeed

a   The online petition _____ in forcing the government to change their policy.

b   My grandfather always wanted to own a small hotel. He was nearly 60 years old before he _____ his ambition.

c   Protestors _____ to throw paint over the visiting politician.

d   Local shops hope to raise $1 million for Africa, and so far they are about halfway to _____ their target.

2 Complete the sentences using a word formed from the word in brackets.

Example   The exam was difficult, but I found it _____ (manage)
The exam was difficult, but I found it manageable.

a   The invention of dynamite was Alfred Nobel's best-known _____ . (achieve)

b   All across Europe we must _____ reduce carbon emissions. (success)

c   Meeting President Obama was the _____ of a longstanding ambition. (realize)

d   Fair trade is only _____ with the co-operation of richer nations. (achieve)

e   After several _____ attempts to find work, Kevin moved to a different town. (success)

3 Rewrite sentences a–e replacing the compound adjectives with a clause.

Example   It was a life-changing experience for me.
It was an experience that changed my life.

a   There are three Chinese-speaking members of staff where I work.

b   I've just bought a bread-making machine.

c   A tarantula is a large, bird-eating spider.

d   This magazine is full of money-saving ideas.

e   The goalkeeper was not really injured – it was just a time-wasting tactic.

4 Read the text below and decide which answer (A, B, C or D) best fits each gap 1–10.

		A	B	C	D
0	(A)	biggest	strongest	largest	grandest
1	A	continued	B sustained	C helped	D preserved
2	A	reply	B response	C answer	D solution
3	A	engineered	B filled	C fed	D powered
4	A	any	B many	C much	D some
5	A	increased	B raised	C grew	D lifted
6	A	difference	B change	C alteration	D warming
7	A	classes	B subjects	C lectures	D lessons
8	A	absolute	B whole	C complete	D total

THE GREEN GATHERING

One of the (0) _biggest_ questions in the battle against climate change is: can our modern lifestyle really be (1) _____ by alternative energy sources alone? A festival called The Green Gathering is attempting to prove that the (2) _____ to this question is yes. Even though the festival attracts about 20,000 people, it uses no fossil fuels at all. Vehicles within the festival are (3) _____ by vegetable oil or grass. Solar and wind power provide the electricity for the (4) _____ nightclubs and bars.

The Green Gathering (5) _____ out of the hippy movement of the 1970s, which promoted an alternative lifestyle. But these days, you don't have to be a hippy to care deeply about climate (6) _____ . It's something we all should worry about, and festivals like these can teach us important (7) _____ about how to make our lifestyle more ecologically friendly.

Watching the bands perform, you'd assume that enormous petrol-driven generators provided the power. But in fact, the (8) _____ thing is powered by solar panels.

Appendix

1 The circle of life

Lead in page 9

3 Scarlett Johansson (photo 1) and Hunter Johansson (photo 6) are twins.

Ben Affleck (photo 2) and Casey Affleck (photo 7) are brothers.

Goldie Hawn (photo 3) are Kate Hudson (photo 8) are mother and daughter.

Charlie Sheen (photo 4) and Martin Sheen (photo 5) are son and father.

10 All in the mind

Lead in page 117

3

What's your **learning style**?

Mostly 'A' answers: You have a visual learning style. You learn best by looking at pictures, charts, films and diagrams. You remember from seeing rather than listening.

Mostly 'B' answers: You have an auditory learning style. You learn best by listening to explanations, talking, and repeating things out loud. You remember things you have heard more than things you have seen.

Mostly 'C' answers: You have a kinaesthetic learning style. You learn best by doing, moving and touching. The best way for you to learn a language, for example, is by interacting with other learners.

10

Lead in page 117

4 Look at the photos and answer these questions.
   a Which person didn't introduce themselves earlier?
   b Can you remember the other five names?
   c What else can you remember about them?
   d Did anybody in the class remember everything
     about each person?

Grammar page 121

5 1 A   2 A   3 B   4 A   5 A   6 C

Writing Guide

Exam strategy

- In the Writing paper, you need to do two pieces of writing in 80 minutes. Both tasks have equal marks, so you should spend about 40 minutes on each one. Time yourself!

- Part 1 is compulsory.

- Read all the tasks for Part 2 before choosing which one to answer.

- Before you start writing, make a plan. However, only spend 5–10 minutes planning each task.

- Each piece of writing should be between 140 and 190 words. Make sure you do not write too much or too little.

- Allow a few minutes at the end to read your work through and check the spelling and grammar. You will lose marks if there are mistakes.

- Remember that to get a good mark you must make sure your answer exactly matches the task. So your Part 1 essay must a) answer the essay question and b) include all the points mentioned in the notes. Your Part 2 answer must a) have the correct structure and style for the text type you have chosen (article, email, letter, report or review) and b) include any relevant information that you are given as part of the question.

Part 1 An essay

In your English class, you have been talking about TV-watching habits. Now your English teacher has asked you to write an essay.

Write an **essay** of 140–190 words using all the notes and give reasons for your point of view.

Essay question

Do children spend too much time watching television?

Notes

Things to write about

1 education
2 physical activity
3 your own idea

Nowadays many homes have more than one television, and some children even have a TV in their bedrooms. It is not surprising, then, that statistics show that watching television is the most popular activity for the majority of children. (a)

There is no doubt that children need time to relax after school, and most children's programmes are certainly very entertaining. Furthermore, (b) some television programmes, especially documentaries and news programmes, are educational and informative, and can contribute to a child's education. (c) (d)

Having said that, (b) many children's programmes are of poor quality, and children learn nothing from them. What is more, (b) watching television is a very passive activity requiring no physical activity. In my view, it would be better if children spent more time on more creative and imaginative activities, and on sport. (c) (d)

To sum up, (b) I believe that parents should limit the amount of time that children spend in front of the television to one or two hours a day. Otherwise, we run the risk of creating generations of unhealthy and ill-educated young adults. (e)

a Refer to the question in the first paragraph and give a few introductory ideas.

b Use linking words to connect ideas and sentences.

c Present both sides of the argument.

d Put the two sides of the argument in separate paragraphs.

e Express your own opinion in the final paragraph.

●●● Phrase Bank

Expressing your opinions
In my view / opinion, …
I firmly believe that …
It seems to me that …

Expressing other people's views
Some people think/claim/maintain that …
It is sometimes said that …
It could be argued that …

Making additional points
Furthermore, …
In addition, …
What is more, …

Expressing a contrast
While that may be true, …
On the other hand, …
However, …
Having said that, …

Summing up
To sum up, …
In conclusion, …
On balance, I feel that …

Part 2 A formal letter or email

You saw this job advertisement in a magazine called *Jobs Abroad*. Write a **letter** of application in 140–190 words.

> ## CAMP UK
>
> We are looking for *Sports and Activities Organizers* to work in our summer camp for teenagers in Scotland.
>
> Write and tell us why you want the job and what you could bring to it, including any relevant experience.
>
> A good command of English is essential, as is the ability to interact with teenagers.

Dear Sir or Madam, (a)

I am writing to apply for the post of Sports and Activities Organizer, (f) as advertised in Jobs Abroad magazine. (b) (c)

I would very much welcome the opportunity to spend the summer working at Camp UK in Scotland as (e) I enjoy working with teenagers, and (f) would also like to get to know more about life and customs in the UK. Moreover, (e) I am a keen sportsperson and enjoy horse-riding, tennis and volleyball. Last summer, I spent two weeks working as a volunteer at a horse-riding camp for disabled children. (c)

I have a good command of English, (f) having studied it at school for eight years, and I have also (e) spent a month at a summer school in Ireland. I am particularly fluent in everyday situations and am confident that I could interact (f) in a free and relaxed way with English-speaking teenagers. (c)

I look forward to hearing from you. (d)

Yours faithfully, (a)

Joanna Murdoch

---

a If you begin the letter with *Dear Sir* or *Madam*, finish with *Yours faithfully*. If you begin with *Dear (Mr Smith)*, finish with *Yours sincerely*.

b Start by saying why you are writing.

c Divide the letter into three or four short paragraphs, each with its own topic.

d If you expect a reply to your letter write 'I look forward to hearing from you.' after the final paragraph.

e Use linking words to join ideas and sentences.

f Refer to the task but do not copy out large parts of it.

g Use a style appropriate to the situation, and maintain the same style throughout the letter or email.

●●● Phrase Bank

Giving a reason for writing
I am writing to apply for …
I am writing to enquire about …
I am writing to complain about …
I am writing in response to …

Applying for a job
I have considerable experience of …
I consider myself to be …
I would welcome the opportunity to …

Requesting information
I'd be grateful if you could tell me …
Could you please let me know …?

Part 2 An informal letter or email

You have received a letter from an American friend, Sally. Read this part of the letter and then write your **letter** to Sally in 140–190 words.

> *After a month by the sea, I was ready to come back to the city. What about you? What did you do during your summer holidays? Please write and tell me!*
>
> *Love*
>
> *Sally*

a Mention the correspondence that you have received. Thank the person for it or react to it in some way.

b Use informal language, contractions, some short sentences, phrasal verbs and (one or two) exclamation marks.

c Divide the letter into three or four short paragraphs, each with its own topic.

d Finish the letter with an informal phrase such as *Love, Lots of love, Take care* or *All the best*.

●●● Phrase Bank

Starting the letter
Thanks very much for your letter. It was good to hear from you.
How have you been?
How are things with you and your family?
I'm sorry I haven't written for ages. I've been …

Finishing the letter
Anyway, that's all for now.
I'd better stop here. I've got to …
Give my love/regards to …
Write again soon.
I look forward to seeing you again soon.

Dear Sally

Thanks for your letter. (a) It sounds like you had a great summer. I really enjoyed the holidays too, but they weren't long enough! (b) (c)

As soon as school broke up I went off to Spain with my parents. We stayed in a lovely little village on the north coast and spent loads of time on the beach or walking in the mountains. (c)

When I came back I spent three weeks working in a café. At first I was in the kitchen, washing up – I hated that. But after a while the boss (b) let me take orders and serve customers. That was much more fun, and I got some good tips too. In the final week of the holiday I went and stayed with my cousins. We just lazed around (b) and spent most of the time watching DVDs. Then it was back to school. (c)

Anyway, I'd (b) better stop here as I've got quite a lot of homework to get through before tomorrow. (c)

How's school going? Write again soon with more news.

Love (d)

Laura

Part 2 A review

You recently saw this notice in a magazine.

Book reviews

Have you read any books recently? If so, please write and tell us about one of them. Say what you liked or didn't like about the story and the characters.

Write a **review** of 140–190 words.

a In the first paragraph mention what you are reviewing and give relevant information (such as the author of a book or the director of a film).

b You can be both positive and negative.

c Say briefly what happens in the book, play, film, etc.

d Put each topic in a separate paragraph.

e Summarize your opinion in the final paragraph and give a recommendation (either positive or negative).

f If you can, give examples to support your opinions.

●●● Phrase Bank

Giving background information
I recently read / saw …
One of my favourite films / books is …

Describing a story
It's set in …
It tells the story of …
There's a twist at the end.
The main character is …

Giving a recommendation
I can thoroughly recommend this book / film.
Go and see this film / Read this book. You won't be disappointed.
I certainly wouldn't recommend this film / play.
Don't bother reading … / going to see … . It isn't worth it.

I recently read The Phantom of the Opera, a novel written in 1910 by Gaston Leroux. It has been adapted a number of times for the cinema and also into an immensely successful musical. (a) (d)

It's set in Paris and is the story of Erik (the 'phantom'), a menacing figure who lives hidden away in the basement of the opera house. He is in love with Christine, an opera singer, but she in turn loves a young aristocrat called Raoul. (c) As you'd expect in a 'gothic' novel, the plot is very intricate with lots of twists and turns, which keep the reader turning the pages. (b) (d)

My main criticism of the book is the characterization. (b) The characters are unmemorable and rather two-dimensional. It is often difficult to understand what motivates them: for example, (f) when Christine chooses to have a conversation with Raoul on the roof of the opera house. (d)

To sum up, I enjoyed this 'gothic' horror story despite my reservations about the characterization. However, I'd only recommend it to people who really enjoy horror or ghost stories. (d) (e)

Part 2 An article

a Involve the reader. You can address them directly, especially with questions.

b Use an informal, lively style. Avoid using a lot of formal language.

c Divide the information into clearly organized paragraphs.

d Finish by summarizing what you have said, and giving your opinion, if appropriate.

e Avoid repeating the same adjectives (like *good* or *nice*); use synonyms instead.

●●● Phrase Bank

Involving the reader
Have you ever …?
What would you do/think if …?
Can you imagine …?
You might think that … , but …

Giving opinions
In my opinion / view, …
I think / believe that …
As far as I'm concerned, …
To my mind, …
Personally, I find / think …

A town that I really like

Have you ever been to the south west of England? (a) I spent four weeks there last summer in a town called Kingsbury, and in my opinion you couldn't choose a better place to spend some time. (c)

Kingsbury is only a couple of miles (b) from the coast, where you can find lots of fantastic beaches. The surrounding countryside is very beautiful and there are some wild woodland areas nearby, ideal for walking and other outdoor activities. (c)

The town itself is very pretty, with narrow winding streets and lots of interesting old buildings. There are quite a few good cafés and restaurants and the shops are excellent. Every weekend there's a farmers' market where you can buy fresh local meat and vegetables. (c)

Finally the pace of life is slower than in the city. People are friendly and they aren't always in a hurry. They have more time to stop and pass the time of day. (b) (c)

So, whatever you're looking for in a small town – attractive (e) buildings, great shops, lovely (e) places to eat and drink, first-rate (e) leisure facilities – Kingsbury has them all. (c) (d)

Part 2 A report

The college where you study wants to raise some money to buy new books and DVDs for the library. The principal has asked you to write a report recommending the best way to raise the money.

Write a **report** in 140–190 words.

The purpose of this report is to consider (c) different ways of raising money to pay for new books and DVDs for the school library, and to recommend the best course of action. (a)

PRIZE DRAW (b)

One idea is (d) to sell numbered tickets and offer prizes. Students and teachers could be asked to bring in unwanted items that would be suitable as prizes, and the school could also approach (c) local shops and restaurants who might be willing to contribute (c) prizes.

SPONSORED RUN (b)

Another possibility would be (d) to organize a sponsored run around the local park. Students could ask their friends and family to give a certain amount for every mile they complete.

MY RECOMMENDATION (b)

I recommend that we organize a sponsored run. Although the advantage of a prize draw is that it would be easier to organize, the plan might come to nothing if we are unable (c) to find enough suitable prizes or sell enough tickets. A sponsored run, on the other hand, is likely to raise more money and would have the added benefit (c) of involving more of the students and staff. (e)

a Start with an introduction setting out the aim of the report.

b Organize the information into sections. You can use headings. You can also use numbers or bullet points

c Use fairly formal language.

d Express opinions impersonally.

e Finish with a conclusion giving your recommendation.

●●● Phrase Bank

Introduction
The aim/purpose of this report is to …

Discussing pros and cons
One advantage of … is …
There are strong arguments in favour of …
The drawback of … is …

Giving a recommendation
I recommend that …
It would be advisable to …
It would be a good idea to/if …

Grammar Reference

Articles

We use the indefinite article *a/an*

1 when we say what something is or what it is like:
What's that? It's a radio.
My sister drives an expensive German car.

2 when we say what somebody's job is:
Tom Cruise is a film actor.

3 when we describe somebody's features:
He's got a long face and a small moustache.

We use *the*

4 when it's clear what we are talking about. This can be because we've already mentioned it:
I've got a cat and a dog. The dog is called Rover.

or because there is only one:
You shouldn't look directly at the sun.

or because it's clear from the situation:
Could you pass me the dictionary? (The one that's on the table over there.)

5 with most nationality words:
The English have a reputation for being bad cooks.

6 with the names of rivers, mountain ranges, deserts and seas:
the Nile, the Himalayas, the Sahara, the Mediterranean

7 with a few countries and most groups of islands:
the United States   the Netherlands   the Czech Republic
the Canaries   the Seychelles   the Maldives

8 in various set phrases, for example:
go to the cinema   listen to the radio
play the piano/the guitar, etc.
in the morning/the afternoon/the evening

We don't use an article

9 when we are making generalisations:
Cats chase mice.

10 with most countries, continents, towns and cities, lakes and mountains:
Mount Everest is in Asia, on the border between Nepal and Tibet.

11 with some nouns following a preposition:
go to work/school   be in bed/hospital/prison

12 with meals:
have breakfast/lunch/dinner

Simple and continuous tenses

Overview

1 We generally use continuous tenses to describe temporary situations:
It's snowing.
I've been getting a lot of headaches recently.
We generally use simple tenses to state facts:
It snows a lot in Finland.
I've never had toothache.

2 We generally use simple tenses for very short actions or events:
The bomb exploded.
We generally use continuous tenses for things happening over a longer time:
We noticed that the boat was sinking.

3 We often use continuous tenses to talk about duration (how long):
She has been directing films since the age of twenty.
We never use continuous tenses to say how many times something happens, will happen, has happened, etc:
By the end of this year, she will have made twelve films.

4 Continuous tenses are normally used for actions or events, rather than states:
Please be quiet, I'm reading. (action)
We normally use simple tenses for states:
These books belong to the library. (state)

Non-continuous verbs

Some verbs are not used in continuous tenses. These include:

1 mental states

believe   doubt   hate   know   like   love
prefer   realize   recognize   regret   remember
suppose   understand   want

2 communication

agree   disagree   mean

3 other verbs

belong   contain   cost   depend   fit   matter
need   owe   own   possess   seem

Some verbs are non-continuous with some meanings but not with others. For example, *think* is not used in continuous tenses when it means 'have an opinion':

I think reality TV shows are boring.

BUT **I'm thinking** about my last holiday.

Non-continuous	Continuous
I feel I should tell her the truth. (believe)	I'm feeling unwell.
My cousin has a Porsche. (possess)	Where are we having lunch?
Does this fish taste funny? (have a flavour)	He burnt his mouth while he was tasting the soup.
I don't see the point of this. (understand)	We're seeing the doctor at 1.00.
Do you consider yourself an adult? (believe)	The council is considering closing the leisure centre.
I imagine we'll eat out. (think)	He was imagining what it would be like to be rich.
The shop appears to be closed. (seem)	Kevin Spacey is appearing on stage in London next week.

Present tenses

The present simple

We use the present simple

1 to talk about a habitual or repeated action or event:
My grandfather runs 3km every morning.

2 to state a general fact:
Koalas sleep more than 20 hours a day.

3 for actions and events in a story, especially when describing the plot of a book, film, etc:
Scout goes to school for the first time that autumn and has a terrible day.

4 with verbs not used in continuous tenses (see non-continuous verbs in previous column).

5 to refer to a future action or event that is part of a timetable:
The next train to Manchester leaves in ten minutes.

The present continuous

We use the present continuous

1 to talk about an action or event that is in progress now:
Put the umbrella up, it's raining.

2 to talk about an action or event which is repeated, but only around this time:
I'm drinking too much coffee these days.

3 to talk about a temporary situation:
My brother's working in China. (He normally works in France.)

4 to talk about changes in a situation:
Air travel is getting cheaper.

5 (with *always*) to complain about annoying behaviour:
That dog is always jumping on the sofa.

6 to refer to a future action or event that has been arranged:
Which country is hosting the next Olympics?

Talking about the future

will and going to

We use *will*

1. to make impersonal, factual statements about the future:
   Work on the new stadium will begin next year.

2. to make predictions based on your own beliefs:
   I'm sure you'll enjoy the play.
   NB We often use *will* after phrases like:
   I think, I don't think, I imagine, I reckon, I'm certain

3. when you make an instant decision about what to do next:
   That soup smells delicious. I'll try some.

4. to talk about future events that are dependent on other events:
   If we leave now, we'll be home before nightfall.

5. to make offers and promises:
   Don't worry, I won't tell anyone your secret.

6. to add a question tag to an imperative or make a tag reply:
   Don't tell anyone, will you?
   'Don't forget your passport.' 'I won't.'

We use *going to*

1. to talk about things you have decided to do:
   I'm going to apply for a better job.

   NB We usually avoid using *going to* with the verb *go*; we can use the present continuous instead.
   I'm going to the theatre tomorrow.

2. to make predictions based on what is happening now.
   It looks like this match is going to be a draw.

The present simple

We use the present simple with a future meaning

1. to talk about things that are due to happen as part of a schedule:
   The next train to Manchester leaves in half an hour.

2. after certain words and phrases, for example:
   when, as soon as, by the time, the moment, provided, assuming, if:
   I'll give Jason his present as soon as he arrives.

The present continuous

We use the present continuous with a future meaning to talk about arrangements that we have made for the future, usually with other people:

I can't go out tomorrow night. I'm having dinner with my grandparents.

The future continuous

We use the future continuous

1. to talk about an action that will be in progress at a specific point in the future:
   At midday tomorrow, I'll be taking my exams.

2. to talk about planned events. Used like this, it is similar to the present continuous for arrangements:
   Next year, I'll be spending most of the summer abroad.

3. to ask polite and less direct questions about somebody's plans:
   Will you be staying at the hotel for two nights or three?

The future perfect simple

We use the future perfect simple to talk about a completed action or event in the future:

By the time they get home, they'll have travelled more than 10,000 km.

The future perfect continuous

We normally use the future perfect continuous to say how long an action or event will have been in progress at a specific point in the future:

By the time he takes part in the Olympics, he'll have been training for four years.

Talking about the past

The past simple

We use the past simple

1 to talk about actions or events that happened at a particular time in the past:
'I left work at 10.30.' Jackson replied. 'I took a taxi home.'

2 to describe a series of actions or events in the past:
Jackson put on his coat, switched off the light, opened the door and walked out onto the street.

The past continuous

We use the past continuous

1 to describe a scene in the past:
It was 2 a.m. but the city wasn't sleeping. Music was coming from countless upstairs windows.

2 to talk about actions or events that were in progress around a particular time in the past:
'What were you doing at 11 o'clock yesterday evening?' asked the policeman.

3 We often use the past simple and the past continuous together to describe how one event interrupted another, longer event:
While Jackson was looking for the right address, a police car came around the corner.

The present perfect simple

We use the present perfect simple

1 to talk about recent events, particularly when giving news:
Have you heard? Tom and Nancy have just got married!

NB We often use the present perfect simple for events within a period of time that continues up to the present moment. Words which often go with the present perfect simple include: *ever, never, just, already, yet,* and *so far.*

2 to talk about an event that began in the past and continues up to the present, particularly with non-continuous verbs:
I've had this skateboard since I was six years old.

NB With verbs which can be used in continuous tenses, we normally use the present perfect continuous, not simple, to say how long an action has been in progress: *'I've been waiting for hours!'*

3 to talk about recent past events that have a result in the present:
You've broken my laptop. Now I can't check my emails.

4 to talk about experiences at an unstated time in the past:
Have you ever been to Rome? I've never tried rock-climbing.

The present perfect continuous

We use the present perfect continuous

1 to talk about recent actions or events that are not necessarily complete:
You've been spending too much money recently. (And you might continue to spend too much.)

NB When the action is complete, we use the present perfect simple. Compare: *I've been writing a novel. I'm on chapter 4./I've written a novel. It was published last year.*

2 to say how long an action or event has been in progress:
I've been learning the guitar for six years.

3 to explain a current situation in terms of recent events:
My trousers are muddy because I've been planting trees in the garden.

The past perfect simple

We use the past perfect simple to talk about an event that happened before another event in the past:
I wanted some pasta, but my brother had eaten it all.

The past perfect continuous

The two most common uses of the past perfect continuous are

1 for saying how long an action had been in progress up to a certain point in the past:
By the age of 18, my grandfather had been working in a factory for six years.

2 to explain a past situation in terms of previous events:
Terry was upset because his sister had been making fun of him.

used to

We use *used to*

1 to describe habits in the past:
   I used to go skating every weekend.

2 to describe a situation in the past that is different now:
   There didn't use to be any shops in this part of town. (But there are now.)

would

We sometimes use *would* to describe habits in the past, especially in literary texts.

> *Every evening, the princess would gaze out of the window longingly.*

NB We can't use *would* to talk about situations in the past:

> *When I was younger I ~~would be~~ afraid of the dark. (… I used to be afraid …)*

Verb patterns

verb + *–ing* or infinitive

When we put two verbs together, the second verb is usually in the infinitive or *–ing* form. Which pattern we use depends on the first verb.

verb + infinitive	verb + *–ing* form	Verb + infinitive or *–ing* form (*same meaning*)
agree	avoid	begin
dare	can't face	continue
decide	can't help	hate
expect	can't stand	like
fail	don't mind	love
happen	enjoy	prefer
hope	fancy	start
manage	feel like	
mean	finish	
offer	give up	
prepare	imagine	
pretend	keep	
promise	postpone	
refuse	practise	
seem	put off	
want	recommend	
	risk	
	spend time	
	suggest	

A few verbs can take an infinitive or *–ing form* but the meaning is different:

1 a) If you **try doing** something, you do it in order to see what happens.
      He tried ringing the bell, but there was no answer.

   b) If you **try to do** something, you attempt it but do not necessarily achieve it.
      He tried to reach the next branch, but it was too high.

2 a) If you **stop doing** something, you do not do it any longer.
      They stopped talking when I walked into the room.

   b) If you **stop to do** something, you come to a halt in order to do something.
      She stopped to admire the flowers.

3 a) If you **remember doing** something, you have an image of doing it in your mind.
      I remember going to the circus when I was a child.

   b) If you **remember to do** something, you do something which is on your mental list of things to do.
      Did you remember to feed the fish?

4 a) If you **go on doing** something, you continue doing it.
      He went on talking for hours.

   b) If you **go on to do** something, you move from one action to another.
      The chairman welcomed the audience, then he went on to introduce the guest speakers.

see (*watch, hear, feel,* etc.) somebody do/doing something

1 We can use *see* (*watch, hear, feel,* etc.) + object + *–ing* form to talk about an action that is progress.
   She saw two men crossing the river. (They were in the water when she saw them.)

2 We can use *see* (*watch, hear, feel,* etc.) + object + infinitive without *to* to talk about an action that is complete.
   She saw two men cross the river. (She watched them cross from one side to the other.)

Reported speech

Tense changes

1 When we report somebody's words rather than quoting them directly, we usually change the tense of any verbs:

'It's late,' he said.   *He said that it was late.*

NB We often omit the word *that* from the beginning of the reported speech clause:

He said it was late.

The normal pattern of tense changes in reported speech is:

Direct speech	Reported speech
present simple	past simple
present continuous	past continuous
past simple	past perfect simple
present perfect simple	past perfect simple
present perfect continuous	past perfect continuous
past continuous	past perfect continuous
will	*would*
shall	*should*
may/might	*might*
must	*must/had to*
can	*could*

2 There are often changes in words which refer to the people, time or place. These are dictated more by logic than by any rules:

'I'm bringing my brother here tomorrow,' she said.
She said that she was taking her brother there the next day.

say and *tell*

1 The object of the verb *say* is always what was said. It is often a clause:

She said she would like to go to university.

If we want to mention the person who is addressed, we must use the preposition *to*:

Would you like to say hello to my cousin?
'You're lucky,' she said to her friend.

2 The object of the verb *tell* is usually the person who is addressed. We do not use the preposition *to*:

Have you told your parents?
They told me the shop was closed.

We also use *tell* in set phrases like *tell a lie*, *tell the truth*, *tell a story*, etc.

Reported questions

1 When we report questions, we use affirmative word order and verb forms after the question word:

'Where do you live?' she asked him.
She asked him where he lived.

2 To report a yes/no question (one that has no question word) we use *whether* or *if*:

'Is it raining?' he asked.
He asked if/whether it was raining.

3 We can sometimes use an infinitive in a reported question, especially when it's a question about our own actions:

'Which shirt shall I wear?' he asked his girlfriend.
He asked his girlfriend which shirt to wear.

'How do I get to the beach?' she asked me.
She asked me how to get to the beach.

Infinitives in reported speech

1 We use the structure: reporting verb + object + infinitive to report imperatives. Some common reporting verbs for this structure are *tell*, *order*, *instruct*, *warn*, *ask* and *beg*:

'Don't be late,' the teacher told him.
The teacher told him not to be late.

'Please help me,' he said to his friend.
He asked his friend to help him.

NB We cannot use this structure with the reporting verb *say*:

We ~~said to him~~ to be careful. (We told him ...)

We can use the same structure for reporting advice:

'I think you should go to bed,' Mary said to her son.
Mary advised her son to go to bed.

2 We can use the structure: reporting verb + infinitive with *agree*, *promise* and *offer*. (Note that we cannot include an object.)

'I'll remember you forever,' he said to her.
He promised to remember her forever.

3 See above for infinitives in reported questions.

Modals

Advice, obligation and prohibition

We use *should (shouldn't)* and *ought to (ought not to)*

1   for giving advice:
    I think you should stay at home this evening.

2   for giving opinions about what the right thing to do is:
    We all ought to use less electricity.

    NB In the negative, it is more natural to say *'I don't think you should …'* than *'I think you shouldn't …'*.

We use *must*

1   for giving strong advice to ourselves:
    I must try to get to bed early tonight.

2   for making strong recommendations to others, based on our own opinions:
    You must try this cake, it's wonderful.

3   for stating rules, especially in written and formal English:
    Cyclists must wear helmets.

We use *have to* to talk about obligation:

> *We have to sit exams every year. (They're compulsory.)*

> NB We use *I have to…* for things that we are obliged to do; we use *I must…* for things that we strongly feel we should do. Compare: *I must start cycling to work. It would be good exercise./I have to start cycling to work. They've cancelled the only bus.*

We use *don't/doesn't have to* for things that we do not need to do. It expresses a lack of obligation; it does not express prohibition:

> *You don't have to leave now. You can stay as long as you like.*

We use *mustn't* for prohibition:

> *You mustn't touch the walls. The paint isn't dry.*

> NB Except for the specific uses mentioned here, *must* and *mustn't* can often sound unnatural; we are more likely to use other verbs and phrases for talking about obligation (*have to*) and prohibition (*against the rules, forbidden, not allowed*, etc.)

Ability

1   We use *can* for talking about ability in the present:
    Can you see that man on the roof?
    Speak up, I can't hear you.

2   *Can* sometimes refers to a future event, but only when the decision is being made in the present:
    'Can you come to dinner next week?' 'No, but I can make the week after.'

    However, we normally use *will be able to* when we talk about ability in the future:
    When she's 17, she'll be able to take her driving test.

3   We use *could/couldn't* to talk about general ability in the past:
    My grandfather could speak three languages fluently.

    However, we do not use *could* (affirmative form) to talk about something we were able to do on one occasion. We use an alternative expression like *managed to do* or *succeed in doing*:
    It was a difficult question, but I managed to answer it.

4   We often use *can* and *could* with verbs of perception like *see, taste* and *hear*. (We can use *could* even when it's one occasion.)
    Pressing my ear to the door, I could hear what they were saying.

Permission and requests

1   We often use *can/can't* when we ask for, give or refuse permission:
    Can I borrow your pen?   Yes, of course.
    You can sit anywhere you like.

    Could I …? and *May I …?* are slightly politer ways of requesting permission:
    Could/May I sit next to you?   Yes, you may.

    NB We don't normally use *'Yes, you could'* or *'No, you couldn't'* as replies to a request for permission, even if the request uses *could*.

    An even politer form is *Would you mind if I …* (+ past simple)?
    Would you mind if I opened a window?

2   We often use *Can you …?* to ask somebody to do something:
    Can you explain that again, please?

    Could you …? , *Would you …?* and *Would you mind* (+ *–ing*) are all slightly politer ways of asking somebody to do something:
    Would you mind opening the window?

Speculating

1 We use *must* for talking about things which we can deduce are definitely true:
He must be tired. He's just run 10 km.

2 We use *may* or *might* for speculating about things that are possibly true. (Some people use *might* when there is less possibility.) We can also use *could* to talk about possibility. However, we cannot use the negative *(couldn't)* in this sense:
Geoff isn't answering his phone at work. He might not be at his desk. He could be in a meeting, or he may be having lunch.

3 We use *can't* for talking about things which we can deduce are impossible:
This can't be Suzie's jacket. It's much too small.

4 When we are making logical deductions about something in the past, we use *must have* and *can't have* + past participle:
I put odd socks on this morning. I must have been half asleep.
Your parents can't have been very happy when you told them you were dropping out of university.

5 When we are speculating about something in the past, we use *may have*, *might have*, or *could have* + past participle:
Police think the robbers may have used a white van as their escape vehicle.

We cannot use *may have* for things which we now know didn't happen. We use *might have* or *could have*:
That was a dangerous thing to do. You might have been injured.

Passives

Use

We use the passive

1 when we don't know who or what is responsible for the action:
My bike was stolen last week.

2 for stylistic reasons, especially to allow the main focus of the sentence to be the subject of the verb:
The saxophone is quite a modern instrument. <u>It was invented around 1840 by Adolphe Sax</u> and has since become an essential part of jazz and popular music.

Tenses

The tense of a passive construction is determined by the tense of the verb *be*:

Most children's toys are made in China (present simple)
This shirt was bought in Italy. (past simple)
By August, the roof had been repaired but the windows were still being replaced. (past perfect, past continuous)
The film will be shown at cinemas next month. (future simple)

Verbs with two objects

1 With verbs that often have two objects (*give, offer, owe, award, tell, send, teach,* etc.) either object can become the subject of a passive sentence:
Jack was given the prize for best costume.
The prize for best costume was given to Jack.

NB It is more common for the indirect object (usually a person) to be the subject of the passive sentence.

2 If we include an agent, we usually put it at the end of the sentence:
She was offered a new job in the company <u>by her boss</u>.

Passive with *know, believe, think,* etc.

1 Verbs like *know, believe* and *think* are often used in passive constructions, especially in formal language, and are followed by an infinitive:
At that time, the world was thought to be flat.

2 If the sentence refers to a current belief about a past event, we use the present simple passive followed by a perfect infinitive *(to have done something)*:
Beethoven is now known to have suffered from lead poisoning. (But that wasn't known at the time.)

3 We can also use an impersonal construction with *it* + passive:
At that time, it was thought that the world was flat.
It is now known that Beethoven suffered from lead poisoning.

Passive infinitive and *–ing* form

1 We can use passive infinitives – *(to) be done, (to) have been done* – in a similar way to other infinitives, for example, as part of a verb pattern or after most modal verbs:
This watch can be worn underwater.
Mobile phones must not be used on flights.
Some passengers pretended to have been injured in order to claim insurance.

2 We can use passive *–ing* forms – *being done, having been done* – in a similar way to other *–ing* forms:
Many celebrities do not enjoy being photographed.
She denied having been given the documents.
Having been identified by witnesses, the suspect was arrested and charged.

so and *such*

1 We use *so* and *such* for emphasis. They make the meaning of an adjective, adverb or noun stronger.

2 We use *so* before an adjective (without a noun) or an adverb:
I'm so hungry!   Why are you talking so quickly?

3 We use *such* before a noun or before an adjective + noun. Note that the indefinite article (*a/an*), if needed, comes after the word *such*:
That's such a lie!   Why are dogs such faithful pets?
You're such a good swimmer.

4 We often use *so* with quantifiers like *much, many, few* and *little*. However, we say *such a lot (of …)*:
I've never seen so many insects!
There's so much to do and so little time.
We've got such a lot of homework.

5 We often use *so* and *such* followed by a relative clause to express a result:
The exam was so difficult that only three students passed.
(OR *It was such a difficult exam that only three students passed.*)
She spoke so quietly that nobody heard.

Relative clauses
Relative pronouns

1 Relative clauses usually begin with a relative pronoun (*who, which, that, whose*) or a relative adverb (*when, where*).

2 The relative pronoun *whom* can be used instead of *who* when it is the object of the verb in the relative clause. However, for many speakers of English, *whom* sounds very formal and *who* is preferred:
The former headmaster, whom many parents disliked, resigned last year.

We also use *whom* immediately after a preposition; we cannot use *who* in this context unless we move the preposition to the end of the clause:
She married the man with whom she'd shared an office.
She married the man (who) she'd shared an office with.

3 Defining relative clauses can also begin with *what*, meaning 'the thing which'.
I did exactly what you asked.

Defining relative clauses

1 A defining relative clause comes after a noun and gives necessary information about that noun. It can be in the middle or at the end of a sentence and is not normally separated by commas:
Did you get the job that you applied for?
The factory where my dad works is closing down.

2 It is more common to use *that* than *which* in defining relative clauses, especially in spoken English. We can also use *that* instead of *who* or *whom*:
I'd love to meet the person that wrote this song.

3 We can sometimes omit the relative pronoun in a defining relative clause, but only when it is the object of the verb in the clause:
Where's the pen (that) I bought this morning? (We can omit *that*.)

BUT *I'm looking for a shop that sells skateboards.* (We cannot omit *that*.)

We often omit the relative adverb *when*:
I still remember the moment (when) I first saw Juliet.

Non-defining relative clauses

1   A non-defining relative clause comes after a noun and gives extra information about that noun. A non-defining relative clause can be removed from a sentence without making the sentence meaningless. It can be in the middle or at the end of a sentence and is separated by commas:
    We spent a few days in Windhoek, which is the capital of Namibia.
    Our neighbour, who used to be an actor, has started a drama society.

2   A non-defining relative clause cannot start with *that*.

3   The relative pronoun or adverb at the start of a non-defining relative clause cannot be omitted.

4   Non-defining relative clauses can begin with expressions like *all of whom, many of whom, some of whom, most of which*, etc:
    The company employs more than 3,000 staff, many of whom are women.

5   Sometimes, the relative pronoun *which* can be used at the start of a non-defining relative clause to refer back to all the information in the first part of the sentence, rather than just the noun before it:
    I managed to visit six different countries, which was amazing.

Reduced relative clauses

1   A reduced relative clause replaces a defining relative clause. We use an *–ing* form or a past participle to replace the relative pronoun and verb.

2   We use an *–ing* form to replace an active verb of any tense; we use a past participle to replace a passive verb of any tense:
    She wears a necklace originally belonging to her grandmother. (= which originally belonged to …)
    The president visited several towns damaged by the flood. (= which were damaged)

3   We can't use a reduced relative clause in place of a defining relative clause if the relative pronoun is the object of the verb in the original clause:
    She wears a necklace that she made herself. (cannot be reduced)

Comparatives and superlatives

Short adjectives

1   In the context of forming comparatives and superlatives, short adjectives are
    * most adjectives with one syllable, but not past participles like *bored* or *scared*.
    * two-syllable adjectives which end in *–y, –le, –er* or *–ow* (e.g. *ugly, little, clever, shallow*)

2   We add *–er* to short adjectives to make the comparative form, and *–est* to make the superlative form:
    long – longer – longest
    If the adjective ends in *–e*, we add *–r* or *–st*:
    wide – wider – widest

    If the adjective ends in a single vowel and consonant, we double the consonant and add *–er*, or *–est*:
    hot – hotter – hottest

    If the adjective ends in *–y*, we change the *–y* into *–ier*, or *–iest*:
    friendly – friendlier – friendliest

3   Some adjectives have irregular comparative and superlative forms:
    good – better –best
    bad – worse – worst
    far – further – furthest

    We can use *elder* and *eldest* instead of *older* and *oldest*, but only when we talk about people (and usually in relation to brothers and sisters).

Long adjectives

We use *more* and *most* for most long adjectives (adjectives with more than one syllable):
exciting – more exciting – most exciting

Adverbs

1 We add *more* and *most* to adverbs to form the comparative and superlative. (Even though we add –*er* and –*est* to two-syllable adjectives ending in –*ly*, we use *more* and *most* for two-syllable adverbs.)
clearly   more clearly   most clearly

2 Some irregular adverbs have comparative and superlative forms ending –*er* and –*est*, as do adverbs which share the same form as a short adjective (e.g. *fast, early, late, hard*):
well – better – best
badly – worse – worst
fast – faster – fastest

than in comparisons

We use *than* when we make a comparison. It can be followed by a noun or a clause:
Steve Martin is funnier than Jim Carrey.
That meal was nicer than I thought it was going to be.

in with superlatives

A superlative is often followed by *in* when we define the group:
She's the most successful student in the school.
It's the most poisonous plant in the world.

more and *most, less* and *least*

1 We use *more* and *most* as comparative and superlative forms of *much/many*:
I ate more than my brother, but my dad ate the most.
There were more people at the meeting than last year.

2 We can also use *more* and *most* to mean 'to a greater (or the greatest) extent':
Consumers are starting to complain more.
Which pattern do you like most?

3 *Less* and *least* have the opposite meaning to *more* and *most*:
I'm trying to eat less.
What do you like least about your town?

4 We can also use *less* and *least* with adjectives (short and long) or adverbs:
We're less poor than we used to be.
Which actor performed least well, in your opinion?

(not) as … as

1 We can use *as … as* or *just as … as* to say that two people or things are the same:
I'm as scared as you are!
Aaron sings just as beautifully as his brother.

2 We use *not as … as* to mean *less … than*:
Cycling isn't as tiring as running. = *Cycling is less tiring than running.*

Subject and object pronouns

When using a personal pronoun in the second part of a comparison, we normally use the object pronoun. The subject pronoun sounds very formal unless it's followed by a verb:
You're stronger than me. (✓)
She's taller than I. (very formal/archaic)
He isn't as intelligent as I am. (✓)

Other comparative and superlative expressions

1 To intensify the meaning of a comparative, we can use *much* or *far* (but not *very*):
That film was much/far better than I expected.

We can use *by far* with superlatives:
This is by far the worst hotel I've ever stayed in.

2 Other common expressions that use comparative and superlative forms include:
The more you exercise, the healthier you'll feel.
Computers are getting more and more powerful, but less and less easy to understand.
The simplest things in life are often the most enjoyable.

Conditionals

General rules

1   All conditional sentences have an *if* clause (a condition) and a main clause (a result). In general terms, the main clause says what happens as a result of the *if* clause being true:
    If it rains tomorrow, we'll stay at home.
    (condition)   (result)

2   We can put either clause first in the sentence. When the *if* clause is first, it is usually followed by a comma. When the main clause is first, there is usually no comma:
    I'd fix your phone if I knew how.

Type 0 conditionals

1   We use a type 0 conditional to talk about a result which always follows from a particular action. We use the present simple to talk about both the action and its result:
    If you don't water indoor plants, they die.

2   We can also use a type 0 conditional to give orders and advice, using an imperative in the main clause:
    If you want to know the answer, turn to the back of the book.

Type 1 conditionals

1   We use a type 1 conditional to talk about a future action, event or situation and its result:
    If you're late, I'll be very angry.
    (condition)   (result)

    NB This is the only type of conditional which always refers to the future.

2   We use the present simple in the *if* clause and the future simple (with *will*) in the main clause.

3   We only use a type 1 conditional when the condition is possible. If it is not, we use a type 2 conditional.

Type 2 conditionals

1   We use a type 2 conditional to talk about a hypothetical action, event or situation and its (hypothetical) result:
    If I were taller, I'd be better at basketball.

2   A type 2 conditional can refer to the present or future. When it refers to the future, it differs from a type 1 conditional in that the condition is much less likely to come true:
    Would you share the money with me if you won the lottery?
    (result)   (condition)

3   We normally use the past simple in the *if* clause and *would* in the main clause. The past tense expresses the fact that it is a hypothetical situation – it does not refer to the past.
    I wouldn't be so upset if you weren't my best friend.

    We occasionally use the past continuous instead of the past simple:
    If they were playing better, they'd have more chance of winning.

4   In the *if* clause, we often use *were* instead of *was*, particularly with the first person, *I*:
    If I was/were you, I'd tell her how you feel.

Type 3 conditionals

1   Like type 2 conditionals, type 3 conditionals refer to hypothetical situations. However, type 3 conditionals are the only type which refer to the past. They are used to speculate about how things might have been different:
    If you had revised, you wouldn't have failed your exam.

2   We use the past perfect (*had/hadn't done*) in the *if* clause and *would/wouldn't have* in the main clause:
    I wouldn't have told him if I'd known it was a secret.

    NB *Would* and *had* can both appear as the short form *'d*. *Would* is always in the main clause, *had* in the *if* clause.

3   We can also use the past perfect continuous in the *if* clause:
    If you'd been watching the road, you wouldn't have crashed.

Mixed conditionals

Mixed conditionals are usually a mixture of types 2 and 3 and refer to hypothetical situations. Mixed conditionals occur when the time reference in the *if* clause is different from the main clause:

If I had gone to bed earlier,	past (type 3)
I wouldn't be so tired today.	present (type 2)
If I were your father,	present (type 2)
I wouldn't have let you	past (type 3)
stay out all night.	

If I weren't going away tomorrow, I'd have accepted your invitation.	future (type 2) past (type 3)
If she hadn't spent all her money, she'd get a taxi home.	past (type 3) future (type 2)

Causatives

have, make, let and *get*

1 We use the structure *to have something done* to talk about things which we do not do ourselves but instead, pay or ask somebody else to do:
Have you had your hair cut?
They've had their house decorated.

2 We can use *to get something done* in the same way. The meaning is the same:
I'd need to get my car repaired.

3 We sometimes use *to have* (or *get*) something done to talk about unpleasant things which happen to us as a result of somebody else's actions:
He had his bike stolen.
Be careful. You might get your fingers burnt!

4 We use the structure *to make somebody do something* to talk about things we cause or force somebody to do:
This film really makes me laugh.
His parents made him clean his room.

5 We also use *make* in the passive to talk about things we are caused or forced to do. However, we use an infinitive with *to*, rather than a bare infinitive, after the passive. Compare:
They made the hostages lie on the floor.
The hostages were made to lie on the floor.

6 We use the structure *to let somebody do something* to talk about things we allow somebody to do:
She never lets her husband drive.

to want/need something done

We use the structure to *want/prefer/need something done* to talk about actions that we want or need somebody else to do:
I need this jacket dry-cleaned by tomorrow.
Would you like your fish grilled or fried?

UNIVERSITY PRESS

Great Clarendon Street, Oxford, OX2 6DP, United Kingdom

Oxford University Press is a department of the University of Oxford.
It furthers the University's objective of excellence in research, scholarship,
and education by publishing worldwide. Oxford is a registered trade
mark of Oxford University Press in the UK and in certain other countries

ISBN: 978 0 19 450284 9

Printed in China

This book is printed on paper from certified and well-managed sources

ACKNOWLEDGEMENTS

*We would like to thank the following for their kind permission to reproduce photographs and
illustrations:* 4Corners Images pp.19 (Cyclists reading map/Fiore Daniels/
SIME/4Corners), 24 (Amalfi Coast, Italy/Simeone Giovanni/SIME), 69 (Cruise ship/
Gunter Grafenhain), 69 (Horse riding/Spila Riccardo/SIME), 93 (Pizza/Pignatelli
Massimo/SIME), 98 (Formal restaurant/Simeone Giovanni/SIME); Alamy Images
pp.22 (Vervet monkeys/Nigel Pavitt), 22 (Pack of stray dogs/Graham Lawrence),
28 (FLPA), 30 (Nick Hanna), 31 (John Morrison), 42 (Radius Images), 46 (Alamy
Celebrity), 81 (girl 5/David J. Green –lifestyle themes), 82 (matches/D. Hurst),
82 (twigs/ICP), 82 (rug/Hypermania Stock Images), 84 (Mobile police display/Ashley
Cooper), 111 (party/Mint Images Limited), 114 (Science Photo Library), 123 (chess/Art
of Travel), 129 (record player/Markos Dolopikos), 129 (typewriter/Jan Tadeusz),
129 (videos/CreativAct), 129 (walkman/GOIMAGES), 129 (film camera/Jiri Hera),
134 (filter papers/fStop), 134 (dishwasher/Michael Willis), 141 (derelict building/
CountryCollection-Homer Sykes), 141 (theft/imagebroker), 146 (youths/Janine
Wiedel Photolibrary); Bridgeman Art Library Ltd pp.52 (Portrait of a man, presumed
to be Leonardo da Vinci (oil on canvas), Anonymous/Galleria degli Uffizi, Florence,
Italy), 53 (Flying Machines, fol. 83v from Paris Manuscript B, 1488-90 (pen and ink on
paper) (see also 162317), Vinci, Leonardo da (1452-1519)/Bibliotheque de l'Institut de
France, Paris, France)/Alinari), 53 (Studies of central plan buildings, folio 17v from
Paris Manuscript B, 1488-90 (pen & ink on paper), Vinci, Leonardo da (1452-1519)/
Bibliotheque de l'Institut de France, Paris, France); Camera Press pp.18 (Girls with
rucksacks/Eberhard Grames/Bilderberg), 19 (Two girls shopping/Dominik Asbach/
Laif, Camera Press London), 75 (Jeep in desert/Fechner/laif), 75 (Saqqara pyramid/
Emmler/laif), 98 (Spanish restaurant/Knechtel/laif), 107 (Kanchana Ketkeaw/Cedric
Arnold), 107 (Scorpion/Cedric Arnold), 142 (Noel Goudin/Perou); Construction
Photography pp.145 (housing construction/Ken Price), 145 (housing development/
Ken Price); Corbis pp.9 (Ben & Casey Affleck/Stephane Cardinale/People Avenue),
26 (Mountain biking on White Rim trail/George H.H. Huey), 27 (Walking through
rainforest/Bob Krist), 68 (First Cast of Piltdown Man Forgery/Bettmann),
69 (Passenger jet/Gerolf Kalt), 105 (Girl in untidy room/Rainer Holz), 107 (Swimmer
Lynne Cox/Patrik Giardino), 108 (Robert Scott and South Pole Expedition/Bettmann),
109 (Robert Falcon Scott in Antarctic Expedition/Bettmann), 129 (tape recorder/
Lawrence Manning), 137 (RoboCup/Indo Wagner/epa), 154 (Smiling young man/
Richard Ross); Corbis UK Ltd. pp.43, 51 (natural history museum/Alison Wright),
66 (Richard Bryant/Arcaid); Dave King pp.62 (Laura-Jane Foley as choir girl in Faking
It/Dave King/Channel 4 Television), 62 (Laura-Jane Foley as punk rocker in Faking It/
Dave King/Channel 4 Television); Eyevine Photo Agency pp.23 (Ivan Mishukov),
113 (Taori roof runner/Ed Alcock); Fat Duck pp.95 (Heston Blumenthal dish),
95 (Heston Blumenthal); Fotolia pp.81 (boy 1/patrisyu), 138 (javiindy); Getty Images
pp.9 (Goldie Hawn & Kate Hudson/Todd Williamson), 9 (Martin & Charlie Sheen/
Jordan Strauss), 10 (Female twins/Howard Kingsnorth/Stone), 19 (Boy playing tennis/
Elea Dumas/Workbook Stock), 21 (Aerial view of town/Jupiterimages), 23 (Ramu, The
Wolf Boy/Hulton Archive), 24 (View over the Vale of Edale/Weeping Willow
Photography/Flickr), 27 (Mountain biking/Markus Greber/LOOK), 29 (Cowboys
herding cattle/Sylvain Grandadam/The Image Bank), 29 (Flamingo flock/Patricio
Robles Gil/Sierra Madre/Minden Pictures), 29 (Woman with lavender flowers/Ligia
Botero/Taxi), 32 (mountain/CSA Images/Printstock Collection), 36 (pensive woman/
CSA Images), 37 (hands holding figures/Ikon Images/Andy Baker), 41 (apartments/
Neil Webb/Ikon Images), 44 (Aldo Murillo), 47 (Burak Cingi/Redferns via Getty

Images), 49 (mother & child/McMillan Digital Art/Photodisc), 57 (face/Wieslaw
Rosocha/Stock Illustration Source), 60 (businesswoman/J. Isaac Allred/iStock
Vectors), 61 (playing football/Imagemore Co. Inc.), 67 (iShootPhotos, LLC), 69 (Couple
on scooter/Tristan Davison and Jeff McNeill), 69 (Bullet train/HO Old), 73 (hand and
seedling/Cargo/Imagezoo), 77 (cruise ship/Linda Braucht/SuperStock), 81 (girl3/
Philipp Nemenz), 81 (Writing postcard/Beth Dixson), 82 (Person standing on rocky
mountaintop/TITUS/Stock Image), 86 (Lake Buttermere/David Noton/The Image
Bank), 86 (College students/Bruce Lawrence/The Image Bank), 87 (Teacher in
classroom/Tim McGuire/Workbook Stock), 88 (Man using laptop/ColorBlind/Digital
Vision), 90–91 (Group of college students/Greg Friedler/Workbook Stock), 93 (Sushi/
Ross Durant Photography/FoodPix), 96 (Cooking on grill/Trish Gant/Dorling
Kindersley), 96 (Ratatouille/Richard Sprang/StockFood Creative), 96 (Baking bread/
Ian O'Leary/Dorling Kindersley), 96 (Roast turkey/Michael Pohuski/FoodPix),
96 (Boiling eggs/Dorling Kindersley), 97 (Slice of birthday cake/Claire Bock/
Workbook Stock), 100 (tea cup/CSA Images/Mod Art Collection), 102 (vending
machine/kel Hiramatsu/Imagezoo), 105 (Woman with shopping bags/Richard
Kolker/Photonica), 105 (Man running up stairs/Rachel Watson/Taxi), 110 (people/
Jayesh Bhagat/iStock Vectors), 117 (Woman in silver dress/Willie Maldonado/Stone),
117 (Man using mobile phone/Bruce Lawrence/Riser), 117 (Businesswoman/Dream
Pictures/Ostrow/Stone), 117 (Man with beard/Martin Barraud/Stone), 117 (Woman
designer in studio/LWA/The Image Bank), 118 (LIONEL BONAVENTURE/AFP),
121 (City/Scott Warren), 123 (windsurf/Ian MacNicol), 124 (students/Jutta Kuss),
125 (Bored man/Laurence Monneret/Iconica), 125 (Hanging wallpaper/MoMo
Productions/Stone), 126 (Hybrid Images), 128 (no time/Owain Kirby/Illustration
Works), 130 (connection/Pablo Blasberg/Ikon Images), 132 (mp3 player/Dorling
Kindersley), 134 (wiper/Grant Faint/The Image Bank), 135 (Statue of Liberty/Travel
Pix Ltd/Photographer's Choice), 136 (stereos/Eastnine Inc.), 141 (graffiti/Darwin
Wiggett), 147 (African lions/Mitsuaki Iwago), 150 (traffic/Todd Davidson),
152 (lightbulb/Creativ Studio Heinemann), 154 (Man using mobile phone/Bruce
Lawrence/Riser), 154 (Woman designer in studio/LWA/The Image Bank), 154 (Man
with beard/Martin Barraud/Stone), 154 (Businesswoman/Dream Pictures/Ostrow/
Stone), 154 (Woman in silver dress/Willie Maldonado/Stone); Imagestate Media
pp.21 (Fall in the Connecticut River Valley/Andre Jenny), 24 (Camel caravan in the
dunes/Jean-Denis Joubert/HOA-QUI), 87 (Family of four at table), 93 (Paella/Foodfolio),
93 (Indian food/Foodfolio); IPN Stock p.11 (Twin boys with red hair/Marnie Crawford
Samuelson); Jupiter Images p.40 (Two men laughing/PhotoObjects.net); Kobal
Collection p.48 (Avatar/Twentieth Century Fox Corporation), 65 (Pirates of the
Caribbean: *At World's End*/Walt Disney); Laurent Laveder p.33 (moon Laurent Laveder
www.pixheaven.net); Lonely Planet Images pp.24 (Serengeti National Park/Dennis
Johnson), 75 (Alexandria Library/Simon Foale); Magnum Photos p.21 (Cadgwith
fishing village, Cornwall/Ian Berry); Millennium Images Ltd. p.147 (Lion behind bars/
Matthew Somorjay); NHPA pp.23 (Mhor Gazelle/Daniel Heuclin), 23 (Asiatic
Leopard/E.Hanumantha), 80 (Asian leopard/Iain Green); Martin Sanders/Beehive
Illustration pp.78, 92; Nordic Photos p.82 (Fire on the beach/Peo Quick); Oxford
University Press pp.21 (Autumn Valley/Photodisc), 82 (mirror/Gareth Boden),
117 (Smiling guy/Corbis/Digital Stock), 121 (Footballer/Rubberball), 121 (Ballet
dancer/Rubberball), 121 (Tropical beach/Corbis/Digital Stock), 121 (Fast food/
Photodisc), 125 (Cleaning desk/Hill Street Studios/Blend Images), 125 (Couple in
cinema/Michael Blann/Digital Vision), 129 (floppy disc/Photodisc), 129 (fax/Dennis
Kitchen Studio, Inc.), 134 (nappy/DKStudio), 135 (remote/Stockbyte), 135 (calculator/
White); Photolibrary p.12 (Illustration of Multiple Earths in Space/Corbis), 16 (man
wearing party hat/Blend Images), 93 (Beef goulash/Fresh Food Images), 96 (Fried egg/
Ingram Publishing), 121 (Lobster/Corbis), 151 (Multi story car park/Alex Hinds/Age
Fotostock); Plane Stupid p.143; Press Association Images pp.34 (metal eater Mr
Mangetout/Ben Curtis), 149 (Daryl Hannah with oil covered hand/Dolores Ochoa/AP),
PunchStock pp.10 (Twin teen boys/Big Cheese Photo), 135 (watch/Photodisc); PYMCA
pp.87 (Club in Ibiza/Catherine Booker), 97 (Lavish banquet/Eleanor Lindsay-Finn),
113 (Free runner performing Parkour/Brian Sweeney); Retna Pictures Ltd p.45 (Katie
Melua); Reuters Pictures pp.34 (magnetic man/Bazuki Muhammad), 39 (gallery/David
Gray), 45 (Monica Ali/Stephen Hird); Rex Features pp.9 (Scarlett & Nino Johansson/
Sipa Press), 33 (swimming/Nick Kelly), 39 (man eating lightbulb/Quirky China News),
39 (fashion show/Billy Farrell Agency), 45 (Quentin Tarantino/Keystone USA),
45 (James Dyson/Geoff Wilkinson), 54 (iron man c/c. W.Disney/Everett), 54 (iron man
l/c. W.Disney/Everett), 54 (iron man r/c. W.Disney/Everett), 70 (Dave Cornthwaite
skateboarding across Australia/Holly Allen), 71 (Dave Cornthwaite with his
skateboard/Holly Allen), 94 (The 'Tasting Menu' of Heston Blumenthal/Eddie
Mulholland), 94 (Dans Le Noir restaurant exterior/Jonathan Hordle), 94 (Dans Le Noir
restaurant interior/Paul Cooper), 97 (Hotdog eating contest/Sipa Press), 111 (formal
dinner/Photofusion), 142 (French 'Spiderman' Alain Robert/Sipa Press), 143 (Mark
McGowan and swan/Jonathan Hordle), 146 (boys running/John Powell); Ronald Grant
Archive pp.58 (Leonardo DiCaprio in *Catch Me If You Can*/Dreamworks), 58 (Still from
Catch Me If You Can/Dreamworks), 64 (Gollum from *The Lord of the Rings*/New Line
Cinema); Still Pictures pp.151 (Village traffic/Henning Christoph/DAS FOTOARCHIV),
151 (Rubbish in lake/Martin Bond); Stock Illustration p.13 (Futuristic cityspace/
Keith00229), 14 (Cyborg head/Joseph 00676), 15 (Family silhouettes/Richard 00883),
73 (Bus symbol/Willie 00234), 74 (City car/Elke 00160), 76 (Man on diving board/
Michael 00182), 101 (Plate and cutlery/Linnea 00691), 116 (Teen girl illustration/Paul
00899); SuperStock Ltd. pp.51 (contemporary art museum/Lorenzo De Simone/Tips
Images), 55 (MARVEL STUDIOS/Album/Album), 81 (Email/Raymond Forbes), 96 (BBQ
kebabs/Mauritius), 141 (homeless sleeping/Socialstock), 141 (homeless begging/
Photononstop); The Stephen Wiltshire Gallery p.119; WENN p.143 (PETA protest
against KFC/Michael Carpenter).

*Although every effort has been made to trace and contact copyright holders before publication,
this has not been possible in some cases. We apologise for any apparent infringement of
copyright and, if notified, the publisher will be pleased to rectify any errors or omissions at the
earliest possible opportunity.*